# Prediction of International Stock Market Movements Using a Statistical Time Series Analysis Method

JEHAN KADHIM SHAREEF

United Scholars Publications

United Scholars Publications, USA

www.unitedscholars.net

ISBN-13: 978-0692498101
ISBN-10: 0692498109

*To my Supervisor Asst. Prof. Dr. Mehmet Bodur / Eastern Mediterranean University, and to my family*

# PREFACE

In this book we have used econometric time series models to model and forecast the development in closing prices of the main international stock markets. These are New York, London, Tokyo and Shanghai stock markets. The time series data set includes the trading days from 1st January, 2008 to 31st December, 2012 i.e. (5 years).

After pre-processing the data to substitute the missing values using interpolation method and converting all closing prices to USD currency, the first attempt of this research employs the Auto Regressive Moving Average (ARMA) framework, which has been used to model a time series data set. It is found that the model can be used to fit the data in the estimation period. The Root Mean Square Error (RMSE) is used to find an estimating order of the parameter in ARMA model i.e. *r, m* proper values.

The forecasting process is constructed based on the ARMA model to forecast the future value for the data indices in the period (2010-2012) in New York, London, Tokyo, and Shanghai stock markets. The idea of forecasting in this work is predicting two-days-ahead closing price based on previous two years closing price for each two days. The forecasting is very important in the analysis of economic and industrial time series, and in selling and buying movement. The money was invested in these stock markets and the results made it clear that the investment in London stock market is the best investment.

**Jehan K. Shareef**
**July 2015**

# TABLE OF CONTENTS

# LIST OF TABLES

# LIST OF FIGURES

# LIST OF ABBREVIATIONS

| | |
|---|---|
| ACF | Autocorrelation function |
| AIC | Akaike Information Criteria |
| AR | Autoregressive |
| ARMA | Autoregressive moving average |
| BIC | Bayesian Information Criterion |
| CNY | Chinese Yuan |
| GBP | British Pound |
| Invp b | Invested capital to buy the shares |
| Invp s | Return capital by selling the shares |
| JPY | Japanese Yen |
| LD | London stock market in code |
| LSE | London Stock Exchange |
| M b | The market of buying |
| M s | The market of selling |
| MA | Moving Average |
| MAE | Mean absolute error |
| NY A p | New York actual price |
| NY p p | New York prediction price |
| NY p r | New York prediction return |
| NY | New York stock market in code |
| NYSE | New York Stock Exchange |
| PACF | Partial Autocorrelation function |
| RMSE | Root Mean Square Error |
| SH | Shanghai stock market in code |
| Shr b | The amount of shares in buying state |
| Shr s | The amount of shares in selling state |
| SSE | Shanghai Stock Exchange |
| TK | Tokyo stock market in code |
| TSE | Tokyo Stock Exchange |
| USD | United States Dollar |

# LIST OF SYMBOLS

| | |
|---|---|
| $y_b$ | Next point value |
| $y_a$ | Previous point value |
| $\bar{x}$ | Sample mean |
| $x_b$ | The next point |
| $x_a$ | The previous point |
| $y$ | The target point |
| c | Constant |
| $e$ | The prediction error |
| $e_{k,h}$ | h-day-ahead prediction error |
| $h$ | Lag of period |
| $\hat{x}_{k+2}$ | Prediction value of two-days-ahead |
| $\hat{x}_{k+h}$ | The forecasting return value |
| $m$ | Order of the moving average part |
| $n$ | The number of data points in $x$ i.e.: sample size |
| $p_t$ | Closing price observation at time $t$ |
| $r$ | Order of the autoregressive part |
| $r_t$ | Daily return series |
| $x_{k+2}$ | Actual value of two-days-ahead |
| $x_{k+h}$ | The actual return value |
| $x_t$ | Current value of the series |
| $X_t$ | Time series of data |
| $x_{t-h}$ | Time series started from $t-h$ |
| $x_{t-k}$ | Past values of observation |
| $\theta$ | Moving average parameter |
| $\mu$ | Expectation of $X_t$ |
| $\Phi$ | Autoregressive parameter |
| $\varepsilon_\tau$ | White noise |

# Chapter 1

# INTRODUCTION

## 1.1 Time Series Data Set and Prediction

A time series is a set or sequence of observed data arranged in consecutive order and in an equally spaced time intervals such as daily or hourly air temperature. Time series data sets are used in many fields such as finance and economy, engineering, and science.

A time series data is called "*univariate*" if it consists of only values collected from a single scalar observation at regular periodic time intervals, such as, the temperature measurements taken from one thermometer, or the flow rate measurements taken from a point of a stream. An univariate dataset $X$ is typically a sequence values $X=\{x_1, \ldots x_n\}$ of the same variable $x$.

If the mean, variance, and autocorrelation of a univariate time series is not changing over the time such data sets are called *stationary*. Many analysis methods apply to only stationary data sets. There are several methods to convert a data set to stationary such as transforming it to difference data, or removing the slope from the data set.

The analysis of time series has got a wide application in areas like population studies, economic forecasting, process control, marketing, biomedical science [1]. Time series analysis uses systematic approaches to extract information and understand the characteristics of a physical system that creates the time series. There are a number of different approaches to deal with time series analysis including dynamic model building and performing correlations [2].

Methods for analysis of stock market consists of mainly two elemental modelling philosophies; Fundamental and Technical approaches. In Fundamental approach, stock market price movements are believed to depend on information about the security, such as the politics, relations to other companies, history and plans, and carried projects, etc. Fundamentalists use numeric information such as earnings, ratios, and management effectiveness to determine future forecasts. In the technical approach, it is believed that all external effects and inner dynamics of the financial object are summarized in the observations of that object. Technicians utilize charts and modelling techniques to identify the dynamics of the object from the trends in price and volume observations. They rely on historical data in order to predict future outcomes and use statistical analysis methods on time series data sets [3].

There are various statistical analysis methods to process a time series data. They can be applied to estimate the future level (expected value), the trend of observations, or the variability of the estimation and observations. As an example, time series regression is used to find out the expected value of time series data, the trend of the data set, and also the confidence level of the expected value. More advanced statistical linear estimation methods such as Auto-

Regressive Moving-Average (ARMA) were developed more than 20 years ago, and they are still in use for accurate estimations [4].

The ARMA model is a statistical time series analysis technique based on discrete time dynamic modelling of the observations by using the weighted sum of previous *r* observations to predict the expected next observation, building an autoregressive model. Moreover, the expectation error is considered to represent the external effects to the dynamics of this autoregressive model, and the weighted average of *m* of past error terms is used to drive the model parallel to the observations. The weighted sum of the past observations builds the Auto Regressive model, and, the weighted average of errors is called the Moving Average part of ARMA [5].

Other than the statistical tools there are non-statistical methods to estimate the expected future value of observations. The field of time series analysis and forecasting methods has significantly changed in the last decade due to the influence of new knowledge in non-linear dynamics. Artificial neural networks are new methods changed traditional approaches which usually were suitable for linear models [6].

ARMA model is commonly used as a prediction model [5] [7] [8] [9] [10] [11] [12] [13]. It gives the researchers the opportunity to forecast the future value of time series data set. J., A., M. and A. [7] applied an ARMA model to forecast the hourly average wind speed in Navarre (Spain) and the result has been proven that the ARMA model is work well for forecasting the future, especially in the longer-term forecasting.

## 1.2 Globalization of the World Stock Market

The globalization of the stock markets is a part of development that has occurred during the recent decades. The following four factors are significantly contributed to this event; i) the advance of technology and increased demand for admission to global markets, ii) the actualization of new banking institutions offering finance casework, iii) trends of liberalization and the decrease of restrictions to adopt ownership, and iv) the movement appears bounded in connection to stock exchanges, allowance and settlements organizations. The globalization increased market efficiency, decreased its accident due to the achievability of diversification, and used arbitrage in an accordant way [14].

Development of internet tools has significant effect on the administration and decision tools for trading in the world's stock markets. The trading decisions are now spread all over the world markets, rather than in local stock exchange markets. In the last 5 years, the amount of investors who used internet applications has been grown rapidly. Also, there is a trend to access to distribute the investment and trading to the global stock markets [15].

## 1.3 Decision Making for Global Stock Market Investments

This book targets to answer the decision making problem for global investments when money can be transferred freely among the major global stock markets. In global perspective, there are a number of stock markets open for investment. The problem of decision making to invest this money to one of the stock markets requires the following steps: (a) a reliable estimate for the two-days-ahead future values of the available stock markets; (b) a decision making algorithm to select the market to invest; (c) the sell and buy operations to be carried in global markets based on the taken decision; (d) the transfer of the investment resources from one global market to another one within one day time.

Most stock traders nowadays depend on Intelligent Trading Systems which help them in predicting prices based on various situations and conditions, thereby helping them in making instantaneous investment decisions [16]. The prediction of the two-days-ahead future value requires time series prediction methods, and based on the literature we have decided to use ARMA method, because ARMA is described as a successful prediction method [7]. In addition, we optimized the orders of ARMA parameters to increase the accuracy of predictions. We collected the market data indices for the New York, London, Tokyo and Shanghai in the period 2008-2012. Considering the effect of the rapid improvements in banking and communication such as the internet banking, and the internet mass media technologies, we assumed that only the previous two years for each two days of this period of time series contain significant behaviour of market actors. Therefore the time series vector is restricted to only the previous two years for each two days when forecasting two-days-ahead market value. For example market value for Jan. 20, 2010 is predicted using time series from Jan. 18, 2008 to Jan. 18, 2010.

In common terms, investment means to deposit capital on financial assets such as bank deposits, bonds and shares for their future benefits. Investment also covers the production of new capital assets, such as education to get certified or to carry out an occupation. In this book, investment is used in narrow meaning of buying market shares for their return rate. Accordingly, the decision making algorithm is simply based on return rates of the stock markets. Basically, the highest predicted return determines the preferred market to invest whole capital effective from next day. The one-day period between the sell-of-shares in invested market and buy-of-shares in preferred market is considered as a necessary time lag due to international banking operations to transfer the capital from one country to another one. For the simplicity of the decision making process the variances and the stock trading volume are not considered to be a significant factor in the return rates. Both of them play an important role in theories of technical stock market analysis, as indicated by many researchers [17]. The proposed investment process is described in Chapter 6.

The proposed forecasting and decision making algorithm is tested by moving capital among four major global stock markets. The buying and selling actions are decided based on the predicted two-days-ahead market values applying ARMA model on the time series data set that contains only the observations for the last two years. ARMA model and decision making algorithm are applied on each market locally, and on four international markets globally to compare the effect of local and global investments.

## 1.4 The Main Steps and Techniques in this Book

The main steps and techniques have been reviewed in this book as following:

1- Interpolation methodology to pre-process the closing price of time series data set (fill missing values) for (2008-2012) period of four major international stock markets (New York (NY), London (LD), Tokyo (TK), and Shanghai (SH)). See Appendix E.1.
2- Converting all the closing price currency to the same currency; USD currency has been used. See Appendix E.1.
3- Converting all the data (closing price) to the return of closing price to induce the stationary time series data set. See appendix E.2
4- Checking 225 ARMA$(r,m)$ models for each stock market to pick the best order $r$ and $m$ parameters with minimum values of RMSE. See appendix E.2.
5- Fitting the data according to the best ARMA$(r,m)$ model detected in point (4) for each stock market. See appendix E.3.
6- Forecasting two days ahead along 3 years (2010, 2011 and 2012) based on its previous 2 years. See appendix E.3.
7- Investing the capital within 3 years (2010, 2011 and 2012) based on prediction values the initial capital was $100. It is Invested the capital in each stock market separately and also in stock market together at the same time have been covered. See appendix E.4.

## 1.5 Organization of this Book

This book is organized into seven Chapters: Chapter 1 contains a general introduction to explain the terminology and the nature of the stock market investment decision making problem. Chapter 2 gives historical information on the global stock markets, and describes the structure of the basic time series prediction method, ARMA, which is used in predicting the two-days-ahead return rates of the stock markets. The source and the pre-processing steps applied on the original daily closing price data sets for four global stock markets are described in Chapter 3. This Chapter also contains the daily price plots of the four markets. Chapter 4 is reserved to the determination of the best model parameters for each of the markets based on the minimization of the root-mean-square-error (RMSE) of the return rates. Chapter 5 contains the details of the forecasting process of the future market prices, and the plots of the predicted prices. Chapter 6 describes the investment process and exhibits the results of the investment which initialized only by a 100 dollars capital. Finally, Chapter 7 concludes on the overall algorithm of time series pre-processing, prediction, decision making, and comments on the possible future topics related to this research.

# Chapter 2

# INTRODUCTION TO STOCK MARKETS AND STATISTICAL METHODS

## 2.1 Introduction to International Stock Markets

This book investigates the feasibility and opportunity of benefiting by investing a capital to global stock markets. The strongest global stock markets available for investment are: i) New York Stock Exchange (NYSE), in New York, United States established in 1792 [18]; ii) London Stock Exchange (LSE) in United Kingdom was founded initially as the Exchange in 1571 [19]; iii) and the Tokyo Stock Exchange (TSE) is a stock market in the middle of Tokyo, Japan, established in 1878 [20]; iv) the Shanghai Stock Exchange (SSE), which is a stock market that is based in Shanghai, China starting in the late 1860 [21].

The daily volume of a stock market is the amount of shares that are traded on any day. The average daily volume of exchange of NYSE, LSE and TS are around $4 $\times 10^9$, $1.05 $\times 10^9$, and $0.14 $\times 10^9$ respectively. The Shanghai stock Exchange volume is missing because it is not announced in the internet, and not listed in Yahoo financial pages.

According to the daily volume of exchange, the significance of the markets are ordered as NYSE the highest, LSE following it closely, and TS is quite a small market than the first two markets. SSE is the smallest market volume, since its exchange volume is about $0.01x10^9 [22]. It is expected that a market with larger volume to be less restricted to global investments, and thus the SSE has a question mark to be taken as a market open to global capital. Chapter 3 is dedicated to the time series data of these major international markets.

## 2.2 Theoretical Background for ARMA

The Auto-Regressive–Moving-Average (ARMA) model for prediction of the future value of a time series data set was proposed by Peter Whittle in 1951 [12], and further improved by George E. P. Box and Gwilym Jenkins in 1971 [13]. ARMA model contains two polynomial parts, one includes the past values of the target variable in an auto regressive structure (AR), and the other one includes the moving average of the prediction error as an input variable (MA). The notation AR(*r*) refers to the autoregressive model of order *r*. It is written:

$$x_t = c + \sum_{i=1}^{r} \phi_i x_{t-i} + \varepsilon_t \tag{2.1}$$

where $\phi_i$ are weighting parameters for autoregressive model, c is a constant, and the random variable $\varepsilon_t$ is white noise.

The notation MA(*m*) refers to the moving average model of order *m*. It is set up by taking the average of sub orders. It is written:

$$x_t = \mu + \varepsilon_t + \sum_{i=1}^{m} \theta_i \varepsilon_{t-i} \qquad (2.2)$$

where the $\theta_1 \ldots \theta_m$ are the parameters of the model, $\mu$ is the expectation of $X_t$ (often assumed to equal 0), and the$\varepsilon_t$, $\varepsilon_{t-i}$ are again, white noise error terms.

The notation ARMA($r,m$) refers to the model with $r$ autoregressive terms and $m$ moving-average terms:

$$x_t = \mu + \varepsilon_t + \sum_{i=1}^{r} \phi_i x_{t-i} + \sum_{i=1}^{m} \theta_i \varepsilon_{t-i}$$

(2.3)

The combined model, ARMA($r,m$) provides two advantages; the autoregressive part (AR) predicts the next value of the time series by its dynamic model, while the moving average part (MA) predicts the effect of disturbances which appears as error in the auto regressive model.

Time series modelling required that the series is stationary. It is stationary if the statistical properties remain constant over time. ARMA model works well with stationary data [23] [24] [25] .

# Chapter 3

# THE STOCK MARKET DATA

## 3.1 The Time Series Data Sets of Markets

In this book, the two-day-ahead prediction of the market prices required time series daily closing prices of the four global stock markets; New York, London, Tokyo and Shanghai for the period starting from 1st January, 2008 to 31st December, 2012, for total 5 years. The data is collected from the financial data accessible on *finance.yahoo.com/* [26]. The original data set downloaded from *yahoo* contains missing days because stock markets are not opened every day of the year.

Missing vectors and values are an important problem in time series data sets when they are used for forecasting purposes, because the missing part distorts the features of the time series. The daily stock market data mainly consists of opening, high, low and closing prices, and the total volume of the transactions in the market for that day. The transactions mean an agreement and communication between buyer and a seller to exchange benefit of payment [27]. All the price currencies have been converted to corresponding United States Dollar (USD) currency [28]. Missing vector means no data available for a day, and missing value means that some of the values of a daily record are missing [29]. Mathematically, there are methods to construct missing data vectors within the range of a discrete data set, such as using previous day or next day values to complete the missing days. A commonly used method to fix missing data is method of linear interpolation, i.e. to complete missing values using the weighted average of the previous and next day values.

For example, in Table 3.1, the value of $f$ for the 4$^{th}$ $k$ value is not available.

Table 3.1: Data with missing value

| $k$ | $f(k)$ |
|---|---|
| 0 | 0 |
| 1 | 0.8415 |
| 2 | 0.9093 |
| 3 | ? |
| 4 | -0.7568 |
| 5 | -0.9589 |
| 6 | -0.2794 |

Previous value method fills $f(3)$ by $f(2)$, which is available in the Table. Similarly next value method fills $f(3)=f(4)$. Interpolation method provides a means of estimating the function at intermediate points, from both previous and next values. In this case, $f(3)=(f(2)+f(4))/2$.

Linear interpolation finds the target $y$ for a value of $x$ using the previous ($x_a$, $y_a$) and the next ($x_b$, $y_b$) values as given by equation 3.1 [30].

$$y = y_a + (y_b - y_a)\frac{(x - x_a)}{(x_b - x_a)} \quad (3.1)$$

Table 3.2 contains sample of the original (raw) closing prices for New York stock market from 17/12/2012 to 31/12/2012 with missing values at 22/12/2012, 23/12/2012, 25 /12/2012.

Table 3.2: Raw data and date of NY stock market

| Date | Closing price |
|---|---|
| 17/12/2012 | 1430.36 |
| 18/12/2012 | 1446.79 |
| 19/12/2012 | 1435.81 |
| 20/12/2012 | 1443.69 |
| 21/12/2012 | 1430.15 |
| 24/12/2012 | 1426.66 |
| 26/12/2012 | 1419.83 |
| 27/12/2012 | 1418.1 |
| 28/12/2012 | 1402.43 |

After pre-processing the data, it shows in Table 3.3

Table 3.3: Sample of data after pre-processing

| Date | Closing price |
|---|---|
| 17/12/2012 | 1430.36 |
| 18/12/2012 | 1446.79 |
| 19/12/2012 | 1435.81 |

| | |
|---|---|
| 20/12/2012 | 1443.69 |
| 21/12/2012 | 1430.15 |
| **22/12/2012** | **1428.99** |
| **23/12/2012** | **1427.82** |
| 24/12/2012 | 1426.66 |
| **25/12/2012** | **1423.25** |
| 26/12/2012 | 1419.83 |
| 27/12/2012 | 1418.1 |
| 28/12/2012 | 1402.43 |

The value of mean absolute error (MAE) with the data (closing prices) which has missing values is approximately equal or higher than the value of MAE when the data without missing values. In NY stock market the value of MAE is approximately equal. In LD, TK and SH stock markets the MAE value is decreased by \$30.048, \$0.4 and \$3.2 respectively.

The time series of the market prices have large movements in mean value, indicating that they are non-stationary in nature. They are unsuitable for ARMA method, which theoretically requires stationary time series data to predict the future values. The logarithm of daily rate of change in prices has zero mean in long term. That means, it is stationary and suitable for ARMA model. It is called *return rates*, *return series,* or shortly *returns*. The return series is stationary in nature. Let $p_t$ and $p_{t-1}$ denote the successive closing price observations at time *t*, corresponding transform the price series $\{p_t\}$ into a daily return series $\{x_t\}$ using

[31]:

$$x_t = \log\left(\frac{p_t}{p_{t-1}}\right) = \log(p_t) - \log(p_{t-1})$$

(3.2)

## 3.2 Daily Closing Price and Return of Stock Market

In a stock market the market price is a result of transactions (an agreement and communication between buyer and a seller to exchange benefit of payment) who have free access to all related information, and do not pay transaction costs, so that the prices change in time only in reaction to new information such as about the predictable return of the security, or about its riskiness, or because of a change in return of investors' risk preferences. A new piece of information establishes a new price level in the stock market, which tends to be continued until additional information warrants another price change.

A single transaction has no effect on market prices since there are many other investors ready to buy or sell small amounts of the security at value very close to that transactions price [32].

Figure 3.1 shows daily closing price of New York (NY) stock market. The random movement of the prices is clearly visible in the plot, where the prices starts from 1400 dollars at the start of the year 2008, makes a sharp bottom down to 700 dollars in 2009, marking the financial crisis, and recovers slowly in four years back to the 1400 dollars level. The shift of the prices in long period indicates the prices are non-stationary.

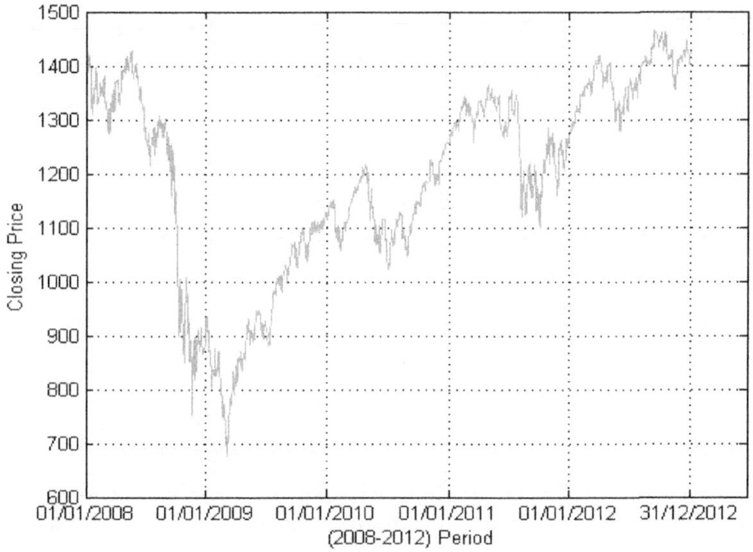


Figure 3.1: Closing price of NY stock market

The return value of the NY stock market for the same period (2008-2012) is shown in Figure 3.2, where the peaks of return occurs especially when the prices starts to raise or fall. The largest positive and negative return values are at the late 2008, during the sharp fall of the prices at the 2008-2009 financial crises, exceeding daily 10 percentages. As noted in literature, the return values have zero mean over the long period, verifying its stationary feature.

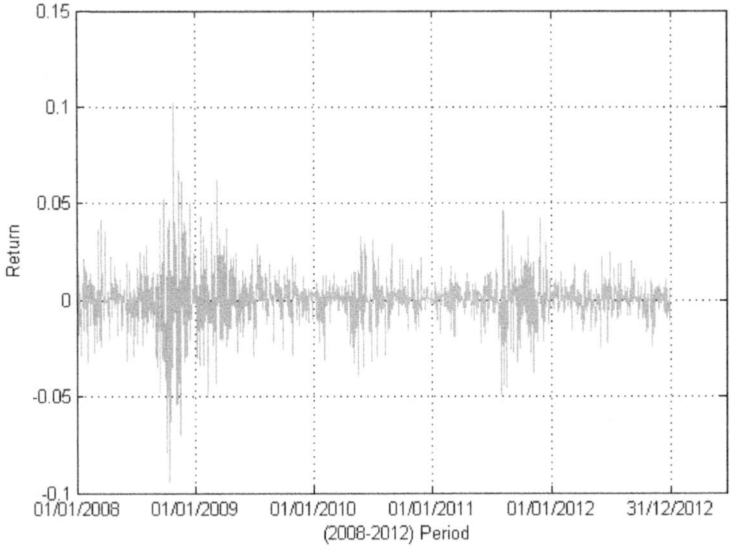


Figure 3.2: Return of NY stock market

London (LD) stock market daily closing prices are plotted in Figure 3.3. The prices initially around 11000 dollars, and resembles the patterns of NY market. However it does not recover fully after 4 years from the effects of the financial crisis. The similarities of the overall price patterns between NY and LD stock markets indicate that they have large number of common actors, and prove that these two markets are global in nature.

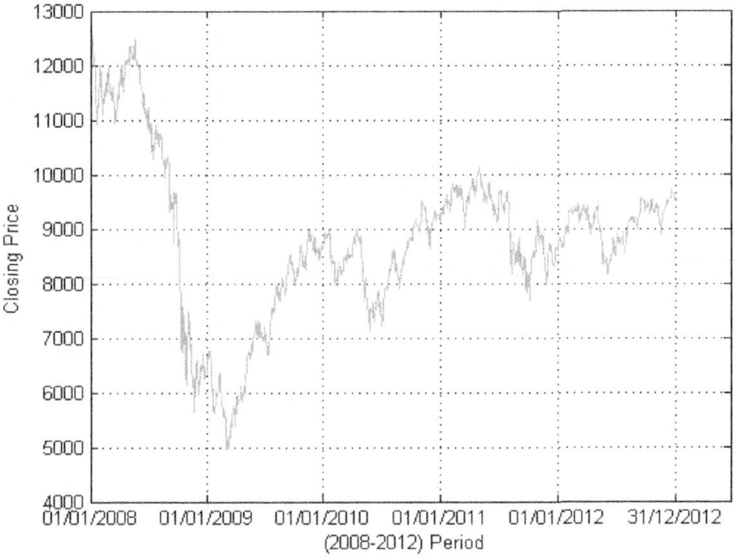


Figure 3.3: Closing price of LD stock market

The return value of the LD stock market for (2008-2012) is shown in Figure 3.4. It has very similar general pattern, even the peak positive and negative values are almost equal to each other, about daily 10 percentage.

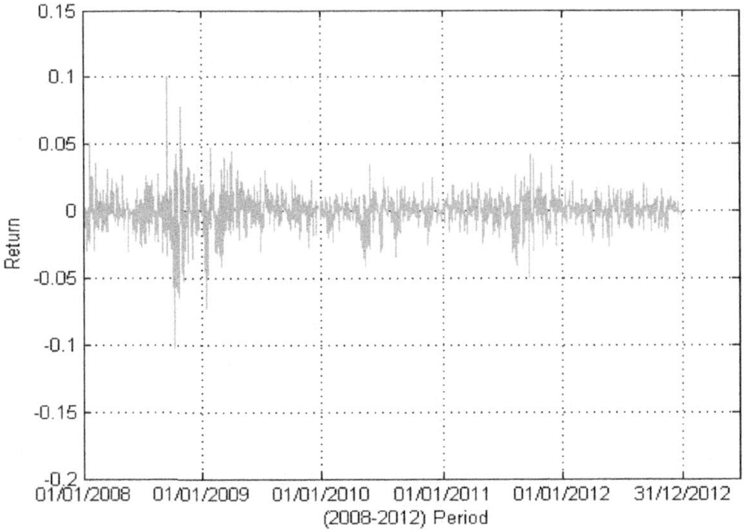


Figure 3.4: Return of LD stock market

For the period (2008-2012), the closing prices and corresponding return values of the Tokyo (TK) stock market is shown in Figure 3.5 and Figure 3.6. Again, similar general pattern is observed compared to both NY and LD markets. The return plot contains significant peaks that do not exist in NY and LD, which indicates the market has both global connections, and strong local actors as well.

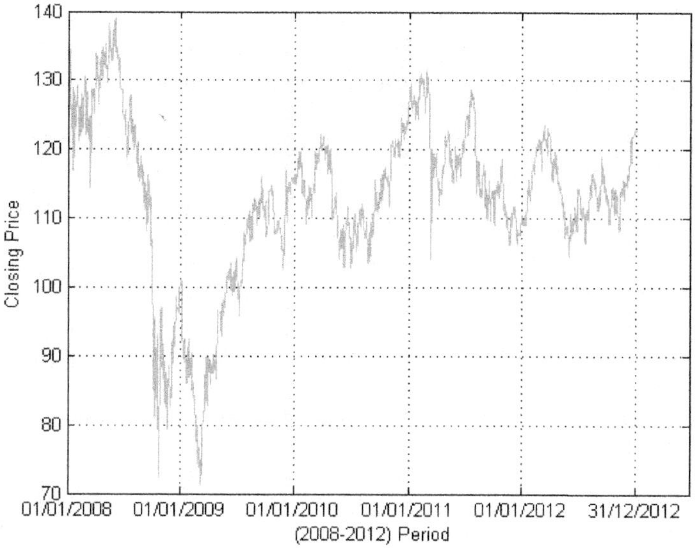


Figure 3.5: Closing price of TK stock market

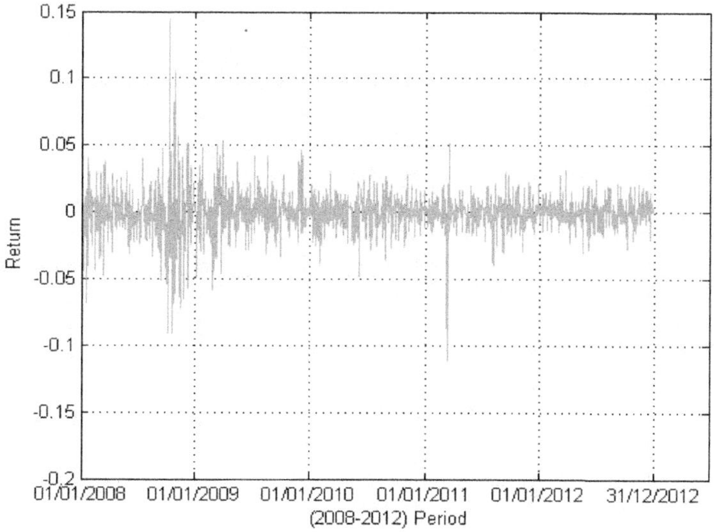


Figure 3.6: Return of TK stock market

The Shanghai (SH) stock market prices plot (Figure 3.7) shows less effect of the 2008-2009 financial crisis, and the peaks in the return plot of Shanghai, which are 2, 4, 6, and 8 percentage (Figure 3.8), are at different days than NY, LD, and TK market peaks. The general pattern of SH return differs from other three stock markets, meaning the market has less global connections, and strong local actors.

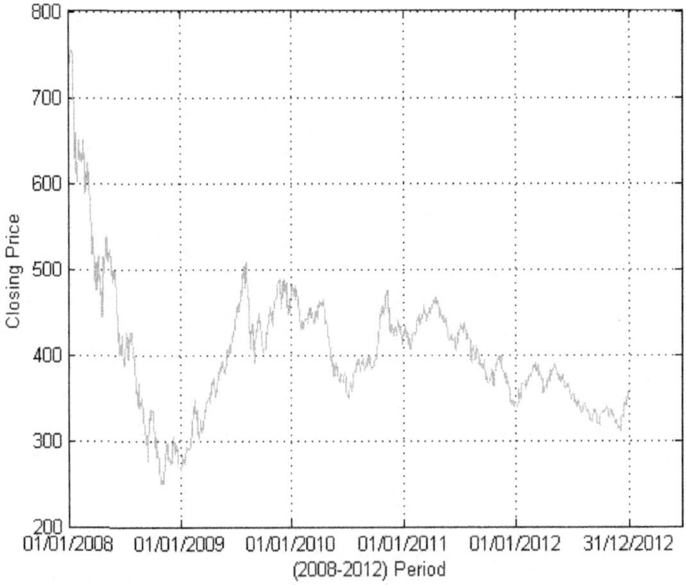


Figure 3.7: Closing price of SH stock market

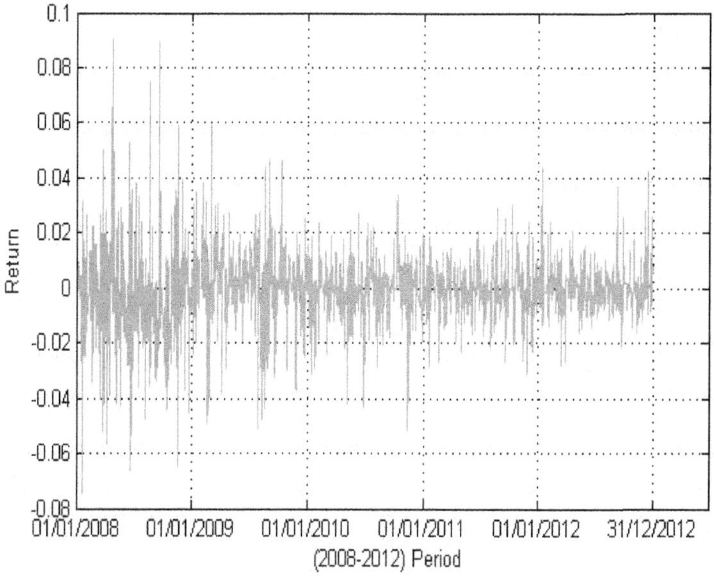


Figure 3.8: Return of SH stock market

In all of four return figures the volatility does not make large movements in short periods. Consequently, during a low volatility period next days are expected to have low volatility, and similarly in a high volatility period, short term expectation of the volatility is high. In all return figures the mean does not change in the long term, indicating that they have a stationary nature.

# Chapter 4

# PARAMETER ESTIMATION AND MODEL FITTING

## 4.1 Parameter Estimation and Performance Criteria

The aim of forecasting in this test is to predict the two-days-ahead return values $\hat{x}_{k+2}$ correctly. The performance of the ARMA model is measured by the smallness of the error of prediction, comparing the predicted value $\hat{x}_{k+2}$ by the actual return of two-days-later, i.e., $e_k = x_{k+2} - \hat{x}_{k+2}$. During the estimation of values for a long period of time, the error may change in positive and negative directions, and their sum $\Sigma_i e_{k-i}$ might stay nearly zero although the magnitude of error is much higher than the sum of errors. Therefore $\Sigma_i e_{k-i}$ is not a performance measure for the predicted values by an ARMA model. The mean of magnitudes of the error is obtained by the absolute value operation, $e_{MAE} = (1/n) \Sigma_{i=1..n} |e_{k-i}|$, which is also called the *mean-absolute-error*. MAE punishes both of the positive and the negative errors, however, it punishes the error proportional to the magnitude of the error. In the most systems and small errors are tolerated to a degree, however, large errors are intolerable because they may result in unexpected hazards. Squaring the error, $e_{k-i}$, makes it positive, and also increases the effect of larger errors nonlinearly as desired in many cases. The mean of squared errors needs square rooted to make it compatible to the output. The resulting performance measure for $n$ successive days of predictions using an ARMA model is:

$$e_{\mathrm{RMSE}}=\sqrt{\frac{1}{n}\sum_{i=1}^{n}e_{n-i+1}^{2}} \quad (4.1)$$

It is called root-mean-square-error, and commonly used in estimation as a performance metrics [33]. The parameters of an ARMA($r$, $m$) model may be trimmed to reduce $e_{\mathrm{RMSE}}$ of predicted return.

For practical considerations, ARMA model shall have the smallest order, which provides an acceptable low prediction error. The parameters $r$ and $m$, which are the orders of AR and MA, are structural parameters of ARMA model, and in the literature, there are methods based on plotting the partial autocorrelation functions for an estimate of $r$, and $m$ [34].

## 4.2 Determination of *r* and *m* by Autocorrelation

The autocorrelation function (ACF) measures the similarities of a series starting from $x_t$ against another series starting from $x_{t-h}$. It is used for predictions. An auto correlated time series is predictable, probabilistically, because upcoming values rely upon present and previous values. The time series plot could be a tool for measurement the autocorrelation of a time series. Positive autocorrelation may show up a plot as remarkably long runs of many consecutive observations higher than or below the mean. Negative autocorrelation may show up as a curiously low incidence of such runs. For computing autocorrelation the relative a horizontal line planned at the sample mean is helpful in evaluating autocorrelation with the time series plot.

In addition, a partial autocorrelation (PACF) is defined to give the correlation between $x_t$ and $x_{t-h}$ after intermediate correlation has been removed. The PACF is obtained from the set of difference equations related to the ACF. Equation 4.2 shows the formula for the sample *lag-h* autocorrelation. For an observed series $x_1, x_2, \ldots, x_T$ and the sample mean $\bar{x}$, the sample *lag-h* autocorrelation is given by [34] [35]:

$$lag\text{-}h = \frac{\sum_{t=h+1}^{T}(x_t - \bar{x})(x_{t-h} - \bar{x})}{\sum_{t=1}^{T}(x_t - \bar{x})^2} \qquad (4.2)$$

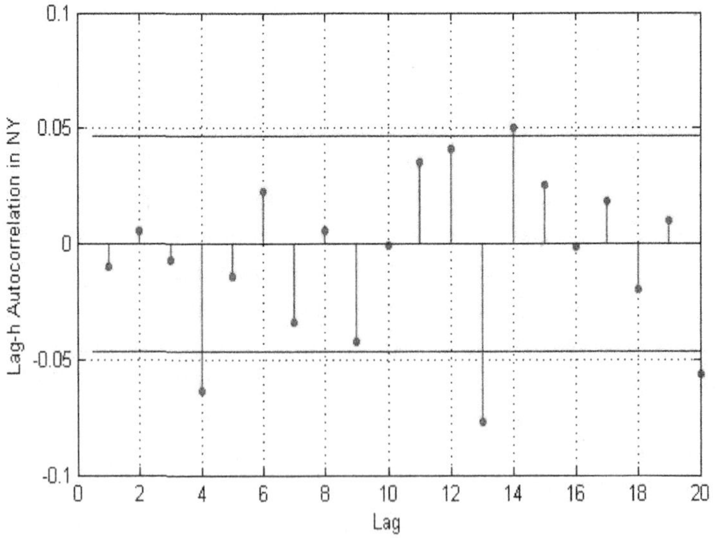


Figure 4.1: Autocorrelation of NY stock market

Figure 4.1 to Figure 4.8 show the *lag-h* autocorrelation (ACF) and *lag-h* partial autocorrelation (PACF) for New York, London, Tokyo, and Shanghai stock markets. These figures are obtained by MATLAB codes using autocorr and parcorr functions. See Appendix E.3.

For four stock markets it is not easily to identify the patterns for AR and MA models directly. For AR($r$) model, the partial autocorrelation (PACF) will be close to zero at lags greater than $r$. For a MA($m$) model the autocorrelation (ACF) be close to zero at lags greater than $m$. As a result, the expected $m$ values according to ACF were 5,8,10, and 14 (Figure 4.1), and the $r$ values according to PACF were 5,8,10, and14 in NY stock market (Figure 4.2).

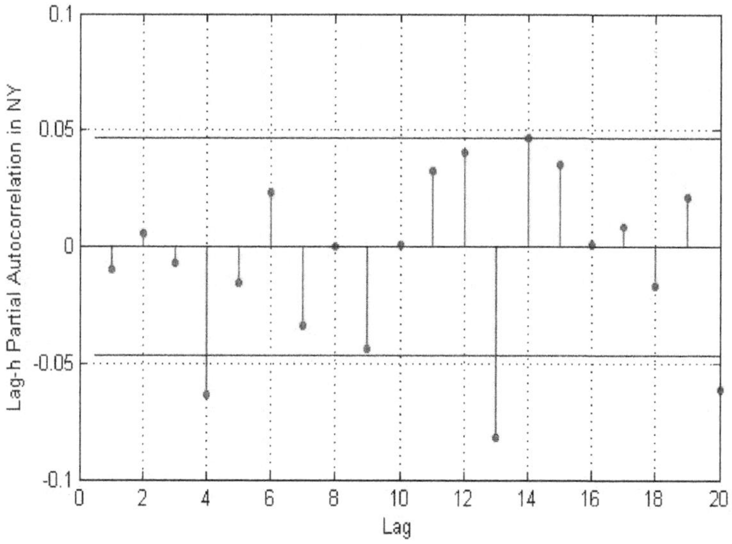


Figure 4.2: Partial autocorrelation of NY stock market

X-axis represents the order of m in ACF and order of r in PACF. Y-axis represents the lag-h of ACF and PACF for the time series data set. Similarly, the expected r and m values according to PACF and ACF are as in Table 4.1 for NY, LD, TK and SH stock markets (Figures 4.3 to 4.8).

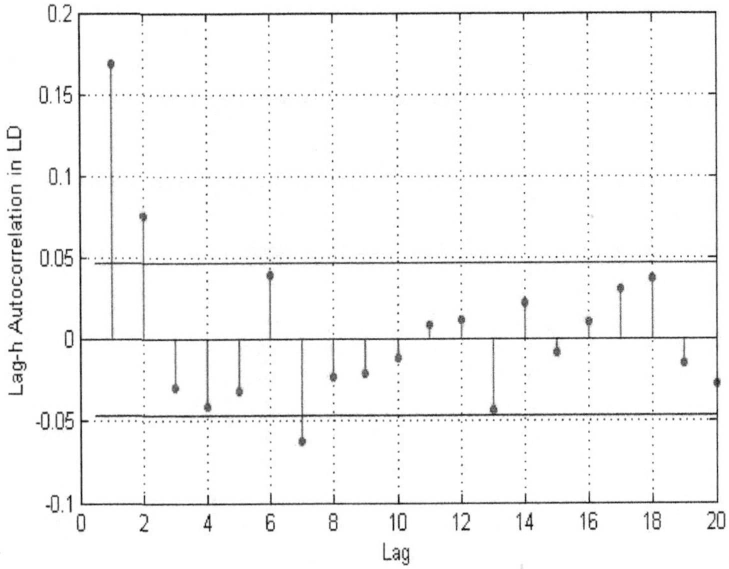


Figure 4.3: Autocorrelation of LD stock market

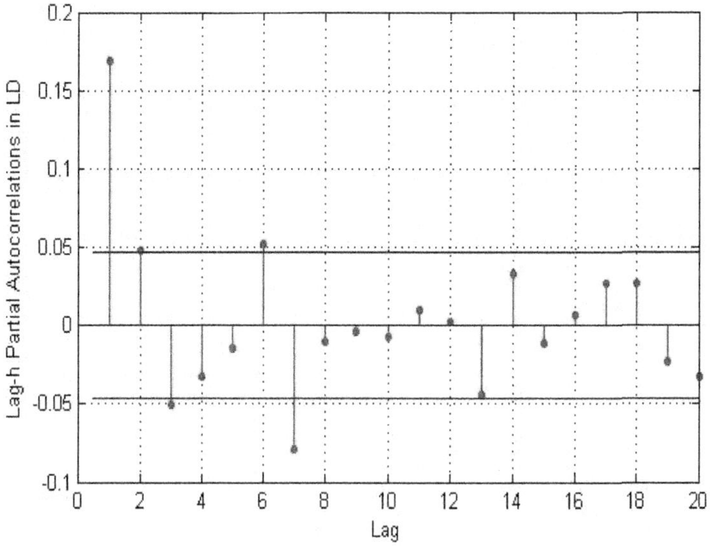


Figure 4.4: Partial autocorrelation of LD stock market

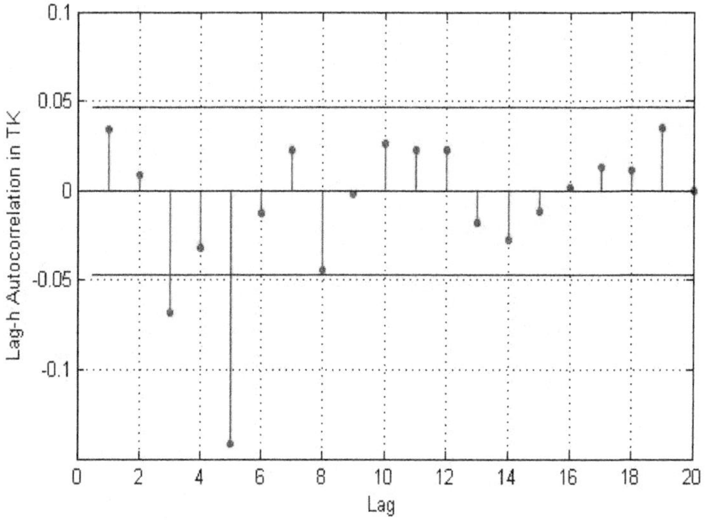


Figure 4.5: Autocorrelation of TK stock market

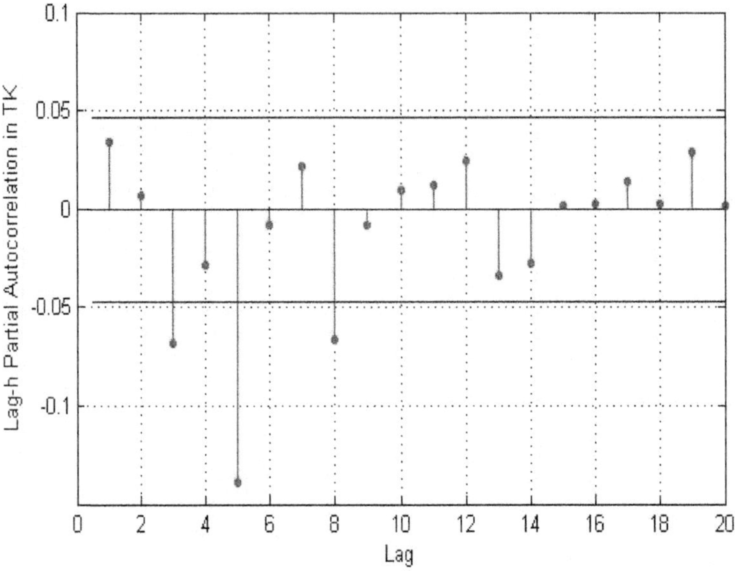


Figure 4.6: Partial autocorrelation of TK stock market

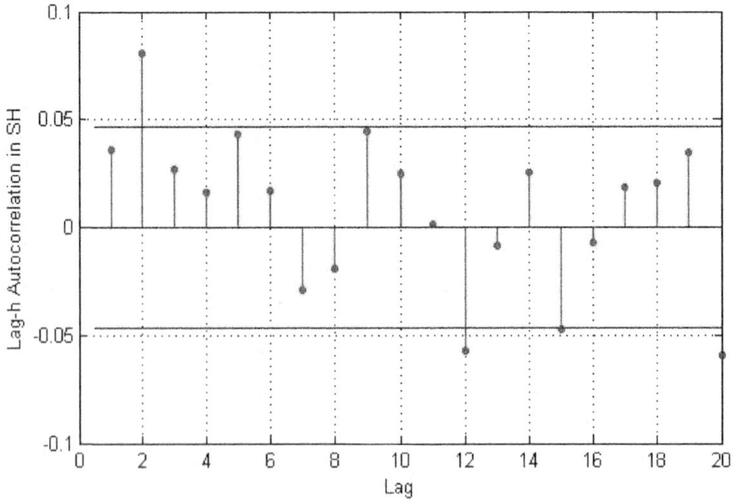


Figure 4.7: Autocorrelation of SH stock market

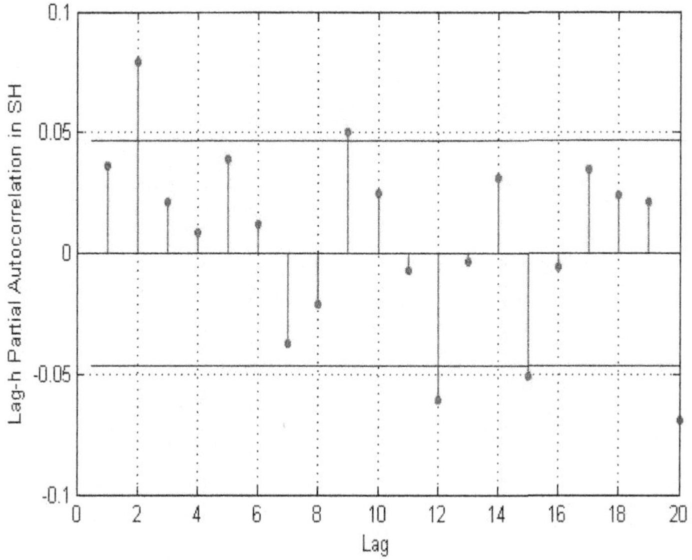


Figure 4.8: Partial autocorrelation of SH stock market

Table 4.1: The *r* and *m* order values according to PACF and ACF

| Stock market | *r* | *m* |
|---|---|---|
| NY | 5,8,10, and 14 | 5,8,10, and 14 |
| LD | 4,8,and 14 | 8 and 14 |
| TK | 4,6,and 9 | 4,6, and 9 |
| SH | 13 and 16 | 13 and 16 |

Additionally, there are widely used information criteria which are the Akaike Information Criteria (AIC) [36] and Bayesian information criterion (BIC) [37]. The idea behind both is simple select the model which has the lowest value of the criteria.

## 4.3 Optimum Structural Parameters of ARMA Models

The time series data sets of four stock markets were pre-processed to complete the missing days, and to convert all prices to dollars, to make them ready for forecasting using ARMA (*r*, *m*) models. The parameters *r* and *m* are called structural parameters to distinguish them from the autoregressive parameters $\phi_i$ and moving average parameters $\theta_i$ in the ARMA (*r*, *m*). The best forecasting ARMA (*r*, *m*) model is obtained by two steps. The *r* and *m* values that give the lowest estimation error are determined for each market data using the root mean square error (RMSE) of two days ahead forecasting over the previous two years data values. The search of structural parameters for the minimum error of prediction provides validation of the determination of structural parameters by autocorrelation model. The ultimate goal of the forecasting is to have sufficiently small error of prediction with less structural order so that sufficiently accurate prediction is obtained by an ARMA model with the minimum possible order.

In the search tests for NY market (Figure 4.9), the correlation of the (*r*, *m*) values determined by autocorrelation functions and the RMSE plots are clearly observable. For example in the partial auto correlation function (Figure 4.2), the 5$^{th}$, 8$^{th}$, 10$^{th}$, and 14$^{th}$ terms (counting them as zero-term+Lag) have significant high values. The RMSE plots for NY indicates clearly minimums at (*r*, *m*)=(5,9), (8,9), (9,10), (10,10), (5,14), (8,14), (6,15), and (9,15). Figure 4.9 also clears the testing (225) ARMA(*r*,*m*) models in NY stock market for all possible values in the range ARMA (1,1) to ARMA(15,15) as parts because of the difficulty of showing all the models in the same plot, in each part x-axis represent the order of

ARMA($r,m$) models and y-axis represents the corresponding RMSE value. All these ARMA($r,m$) models and related figures are obtained by MATLAB codes. See Appendix E.2.

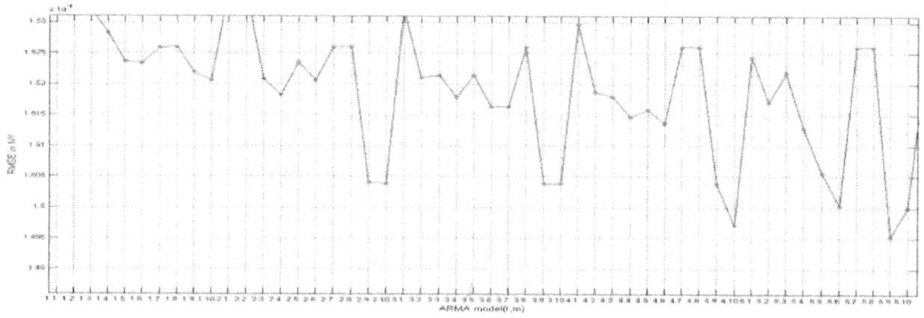

X-axis represents ARMA from (1, 1) to (5, 10) models.
Y-axis represents RMSE value for these models.

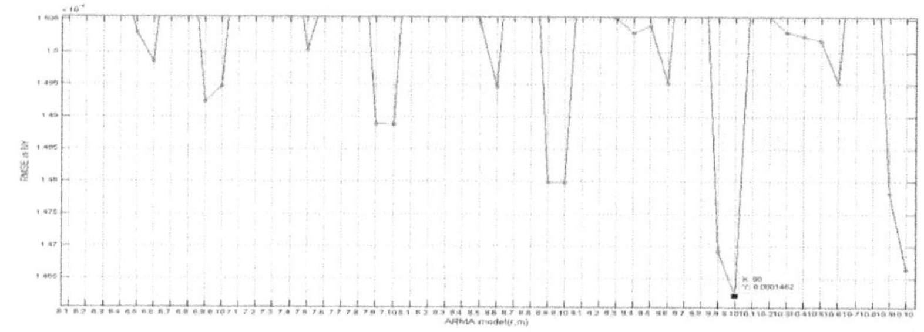

X-axis represents ARMA model from (6, 1) to (10,10)

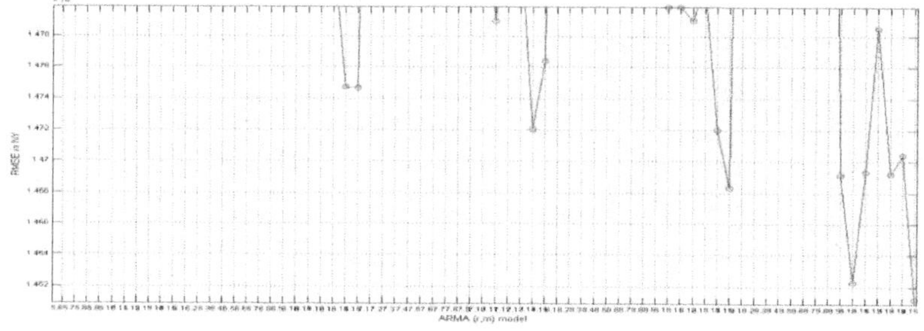

X-axis represents ARMA model from (7, 11) to (9,15)

Figure 4.9: The ARMA($r,m$) model and RMSE value for NY stock market.

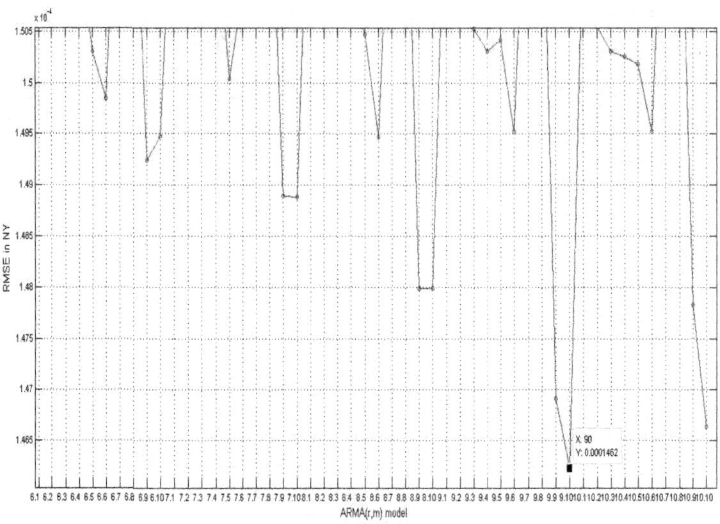


Figure 4.10: Best ARMA(r,m) model and RMSE value for NY stock market

In this work, the best ARMA($r,m$) model corresponding to minimum RMSE value in NY stock market is ARMA(9,10) with $1.46 \times 10^{-4}$ RMSE value (Figure 4.10).

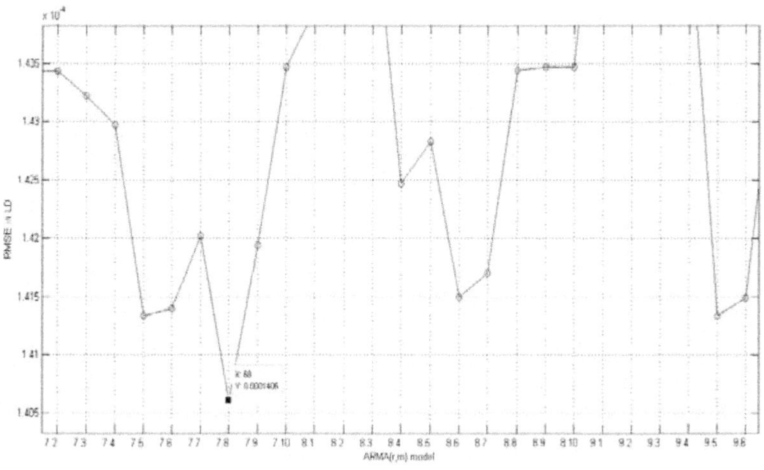


Figure 4.11: Best ARMA($r,m$) model and RMSE value for LD stock market

The two days ahead prediction RMSE plots for LD, TK, and SH markets for all possible ($r,m$) values are showing in Figures (4.11 to 4.13), where the value of structural parameters for minimum RMSE are detected accordingly. Consequently, for the LD, TK, and SH stock markets, the optimum ($r$, $m$) and return-RMSE values are (7,8), $1.4\text{x}10^{-4}$ for LD,(10,10) , $2\text{x}10^{-4}$ for TK, and (9,10), $1.6\text{x}10^{-4}$ for SH.

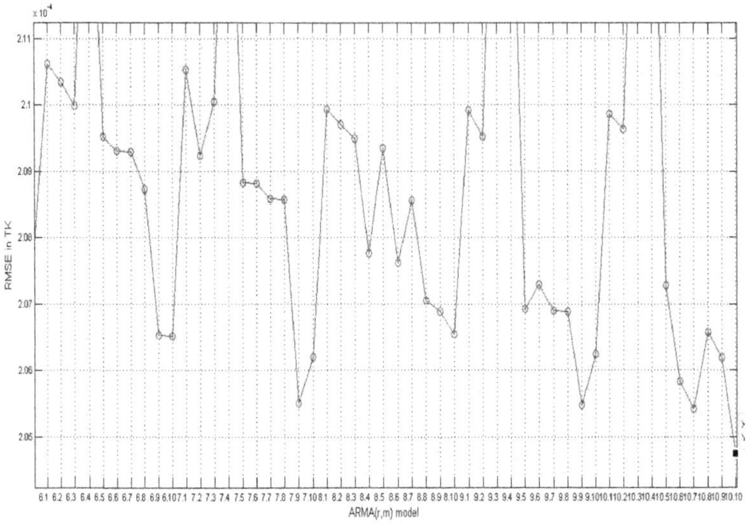


Figure 4.12: Best ARMA(r,m) model and RMSE value for TK stock market

Particularly, the favorite model is the model which has a minimum number of parameters to avoid the large number of computational steps as much as possible, abolish increase the percentage of error and to get close to the prediction accuracy.

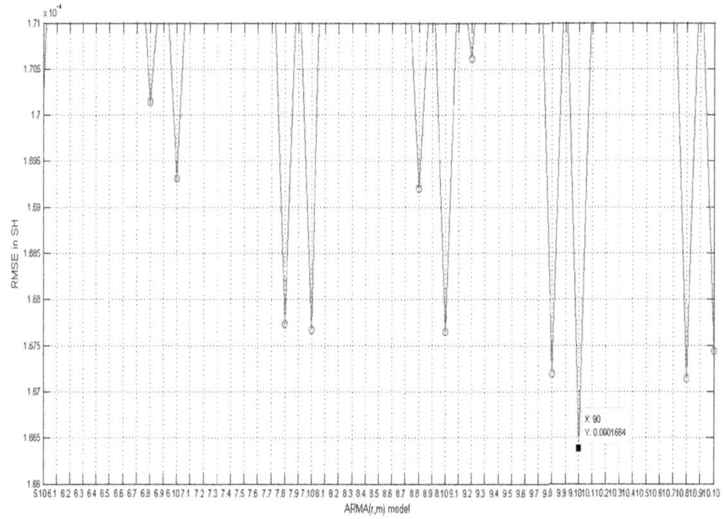


Figure 4.13: Best ARMA($r,m$) model and RMSE value for SH stock market

The next Chapter explains the results of the forecasted closing prices using the ARMA($r,m$) model with the best $r$ and $m$ values.

# Chapter 5

# FORECASTING

## 5.1 Forecasting

Estimation of the future using the trend and patterns in a set of available observations means forecasting. In the finance sector, forecasting is used by actors to allocate their resources for a future period of time. The forecasting of economic and industrial time series is important as a tool of analysis for the business decisions such as selling or buying in the markets [24] [38]. As a scientific technique, forecasting helps organizations for decision making in the state of uncertainty.

Model based forecasting assumes that the system changes states by the inputs, and the states are reflected to outputs by the inner dynamics of the system. Once the model parameters are correctly estimated, the trend and future value is easily forecasted by using the model.

For this research, the objective period consists of the years from 2008, to 2012, inclusive. The observations are collected as the time series of closing prices of New York, London, Tokyo and Shanghai stock markets, all converted to dollars after filling the missing values by method of interpolation, and then converted to daily return values to obtain a stationary time series, which is suitable for an ARMA model.

The h-day-ahead prediction error is $e_{k,h} = x_{k+h} - \hat{x}_{k+h}$, where $x_{k+h}$ is the actual return value at the end of h-days and $\hat{x}_{k+h}$ is the forecasted return value by ARMA model.

## 5.2 Dependence of Future Market Value to the Past

There are scholars, who claim that markets are illogical and influenced by psychological factors [39]. Taleb (2008) argues harshly against the idea that someone is able to forecast the future [40]. In his book the "Black Swan" he argues that financial markets are simply impossible to predict before they happen.

Rational expectation theory is against this view. Valid assumptions in the rational expectation theory states that: a) the random disturbances are normally distributed; b) Certainty equivalents exist for the variables to be predicted; c) the equations of the system, including the expectations formulas, are linear. Starting with these assumptions, the rational expectation theory states that expectation of the future value is significant, even with restricted economic information. Moreover, any speculative action after prediction of the future values reduces the variance of the market prices, and improves its predictability [41]. Accordingly, the linear dynamic ARMA model, which processes the time series data, is suitable for prediction of the future values with a sufficiently low variance.

## 5.3 The Results of Forecasting Using ARMA Model

In this book, the forecasting of two-days-ahead return is obtained by training the ARMA($r,m$) model for each forecasted day by using its previous two years stock market data. Although the parameter values of each day's ARMA model are similar to each other they are calculated particular for that day. Once the estimation errors $e_{t-i}$ are calculated from the previous actual values and their estimated by $e_{t-i}= x_{t-i} - \hat{x}_{t-i}$, the future values $\hat{e}_{xt}$ is predicted by ARMA model with an error $e_t$ by the relation:

$$\hat{x}_t = x_t - \varepsilon_t = \mu + \sum_{i=1}^{r} \phi_i x_{t-i} + \sum_{i=1}^{m} \theta_i \varepsilon_{t-i}, \quad (5.1)$$

where $r$ and $m$ were determined for NYSE as $r$=9 and $m$=10.

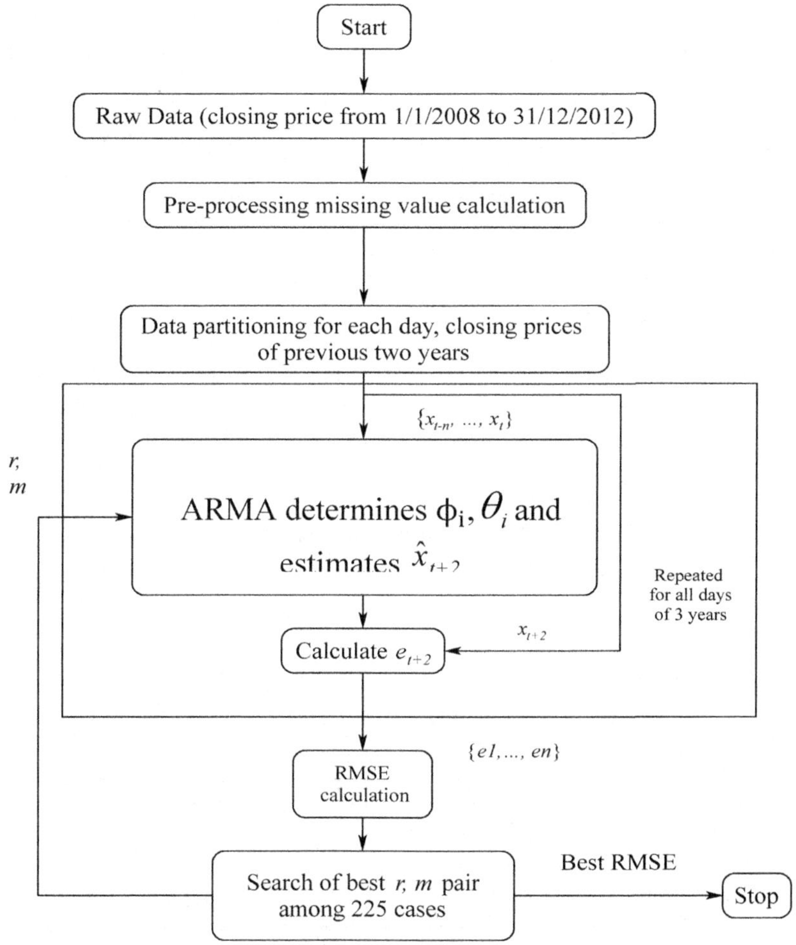


Figure 5.1: Block diagram for selecting the best ARMA($r,m$)model

As shown in the Figure 5.1 two years data is prepared for predicting each day of three years period and the ARMA parameters are calculated for each day. We obtain for each day a different set of values for $\phi_i, \theta_i$ coefficients; however they are mostly very close to each other. As an example of typical parameter values for NYSE to forecast the day (31/12/2012), $\mu$ is 1177.362, Table 5.1 shows the values of $\phi_i$ for i=1...9, $\theta_i$ for i=1...10 and also contains the values of $\varepsilon_{t-i}$ and $x_{t-i}$ for the same forecasting day. The estimation expression by ARMA(9,10) model is written using these parameters as following:

$$\hat{x}_t = 1177.362 - 0.7809x_{t-1} + 0.7303x_{t-2} + 0.5239x_{t-3} - 0.1764x_{t-4} - 0.1941x_{t-5} - 0.0348x_{t-6} - 0.0165x_{t-7} - 0.0081x_{t-8} - 0.009x_{t-9} + 1.9754\varepsilon_{t-1} + 1.5\varepsilon_{t-2} + \varepsilon_{t-3} + 0.9997\varepsilon_{t-4} + \varepsilon_{t-5} + \varepsilon_{t-6} + \varepsilon_{t-7} + \varepsilon_{t-8} + 0.8476\varepsilon_{t-9} + 0.3306\varepsilon_{t-10}.$$

Table 5.1: The $x_{t-i}$, $\phi_i$, $\varepsilon_{t-i}$, and $\theta_i$ values

| Time lag (days) | Closing price and estimation error | | ARMA parameters | |
|---|---|---|---|---|
| $i$ | $x_{t-i}$ | $\varepsilon_{t-i}$ | $\phi_i$ | $\theta_i$ |
| 1 | 1427.823 | 4.823691 | -0.7809 | 1.9754 |
| 2 | 1426.66 | 19.01754 | 0.7303 | 1.5 |
| 3 | 1423.245 | 12.05432 | 0.5239 | 1 |
| 4 | 1419.83 | 16.55566 | -0.1764 | 0.9997 |
| 5 | 1418.1 | 15.04184 | -0.1941 | 1 |
| 6 | 1402.43 | 14.94693 | -0.0348 | 1 |
| 7 | 1410.35 | 21.99996 | -0.0165 | 1 |
| 8 | 1418.27 | 3.343305 | -0.0081 | 1 |
| 9 | 1426.19 | 28.26329 | -0.009 | 0.8476 |
| 10 | | 25.79558 | | 0.3306 |

Figure 5.2 shows the two-days-ahead forecasting prices for NY stock market from (1/1/2010) to (31/12/2012). Figure 5.3 shows the closing price absolute prediction error in NY stock market for the same three years, x-axis denoted to the period from 2010 to 2012 and y-axis represents the error value in NY closing price. The mean absolute error was less than 15.5 while closing prices were around \$1200 in NY; 103.4 while closing prices were \$9000 in LD; in TK the mean absolute error was less than 0.5 while closing prices were \$120; in SH was less than 1.6 while closing prices were \$500. Figure 5.3 shows the closing prices and two-days-ahead forecasting prices using ARMA (9, 10) model for NY stock market on the same plot, in this figure x-axis represents the period in range (2008-2012) and y-axis refers to closing price by USD. However, because the forecasting prices are very close to the actual prices, the difference is not distinguishable on the plot. See appendix E.3.

Figure 5.2: ARMA (9,10) forecasting price for 3 years of NY stock market

For NY stock market as an example of the forecasting value and absolute prediction error of forecasting, on (03/01/2010), the actual closing price was =1128.5175 and forecasted price was =1138.8, the absolute prediction error is $e_{p,t} = | P_t - \hat{P}_t | = 10.2$.

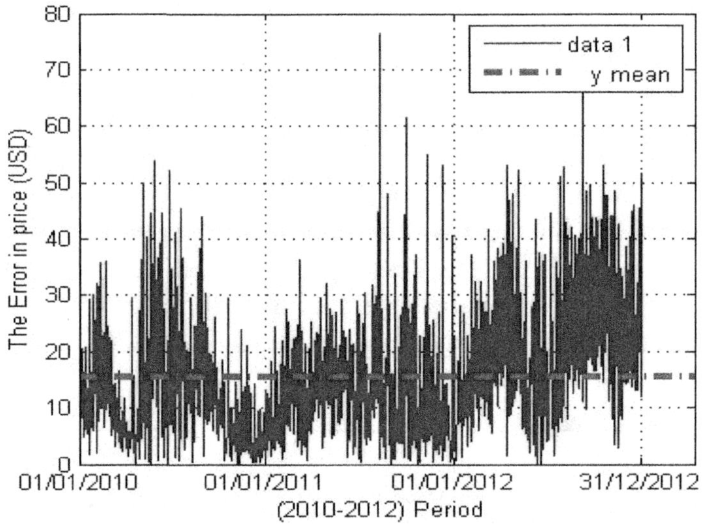


Figure 5.3: The closing price absolute prediction error in NY stock market

Trying to forecast the future closing price in these stock market depending on the raw data which has missing values, the mean absolute error was 15 in NY stock market; 133.448 in LD; in TK the mean absolute error was 0.933 and in SH was 3.745 (Table 5.2). It is clear that the MAE is approximately equal or higher than the values of mean absolute error in the data without missing values, so the forecasting process in this work depending on the data set after pre-processing it i.e. the data without missing values.

Table 5.2: MAE for the data sets with and without missing values

| | NYSE | LSE | TSE | SSE |
|---|---|---|---|---|
| MAE with missing values. | 15 | 133.448 | 0.933 | 3.745 |
| MAE without missing val. | 15.5 | 103.4 | 0.5 | 1.6 |

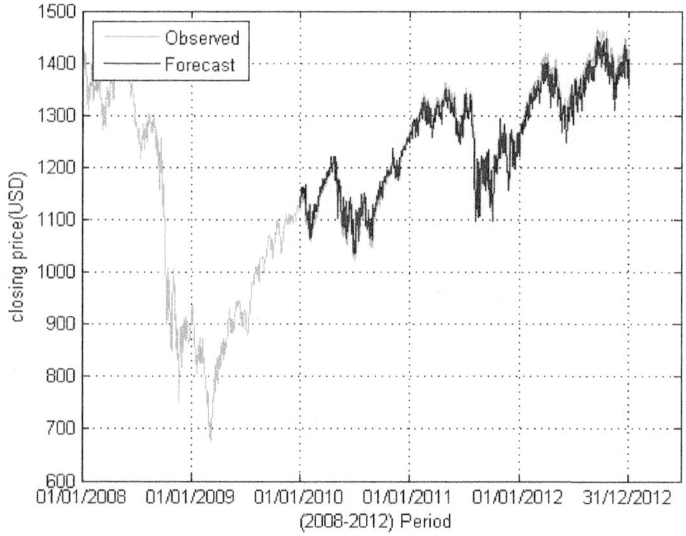


Figure 5.4: ARMA (9, 10) closing and forecasting price for 3 years in NY

Figures (5.4, 5.5, 5.7, and 5.9) show the five years closing prices and the three year forecasted prices of NY, LD, TK, and SH stock markets on the same plots. The forecasting process started from 2010 because each two days are forecasted depending on the previous 2 years belonging to these two days. See appendix C.

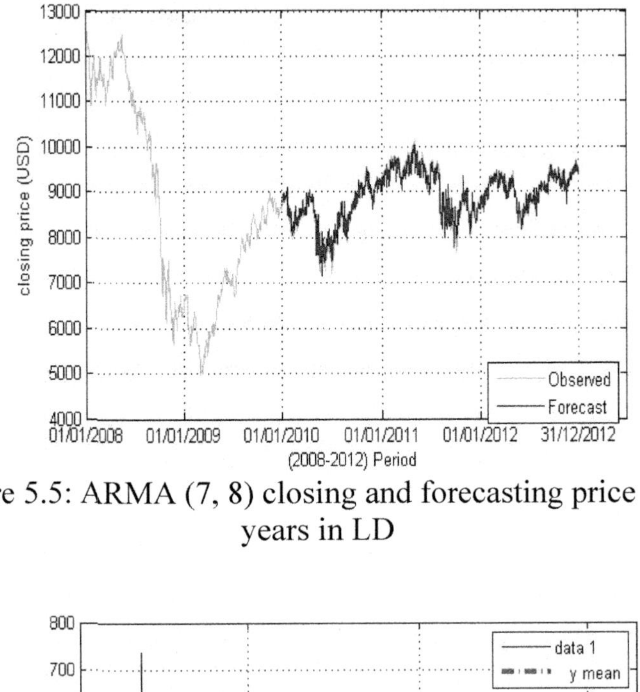


Figure 5.5: ARMA (7, 8) closing and forecasting price for 3 years in LD

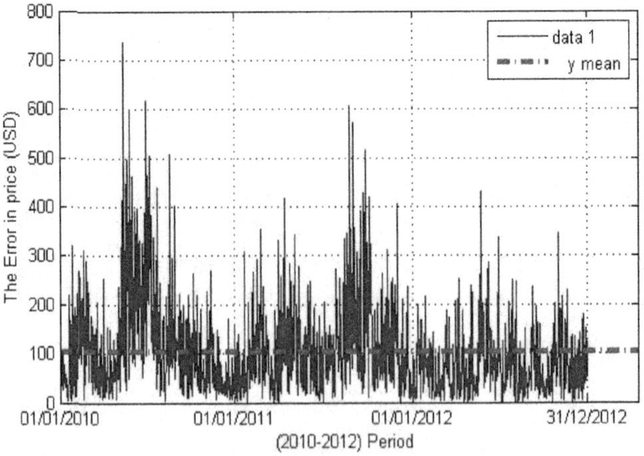


Figure 5.6: The closing price absolute prediction error in LD stock market

Figures (5.6, 5.8, and 5.10) refer to the absolute prediction error of LD, TK, and SH stock markets.

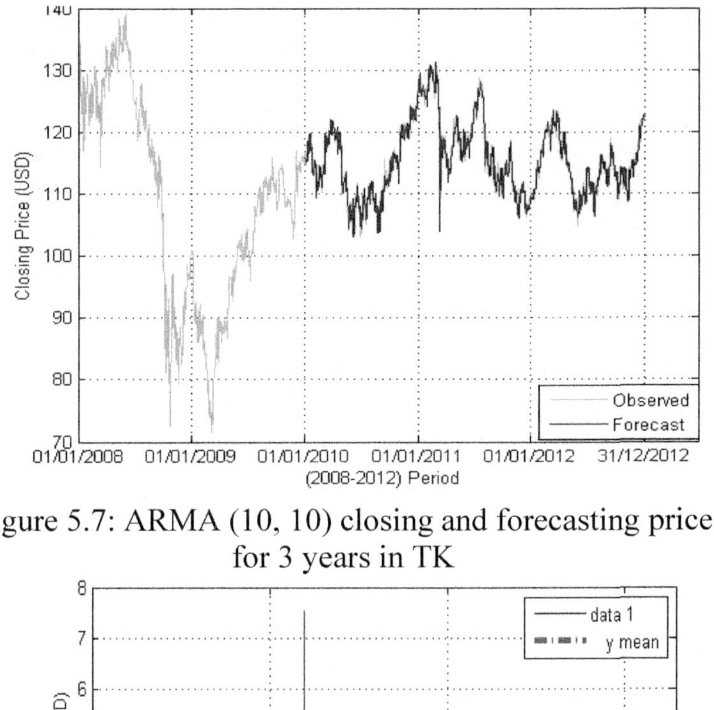


Figure 5.7: ARMA (10, 10) closing and forecasting price for 3 years in TK

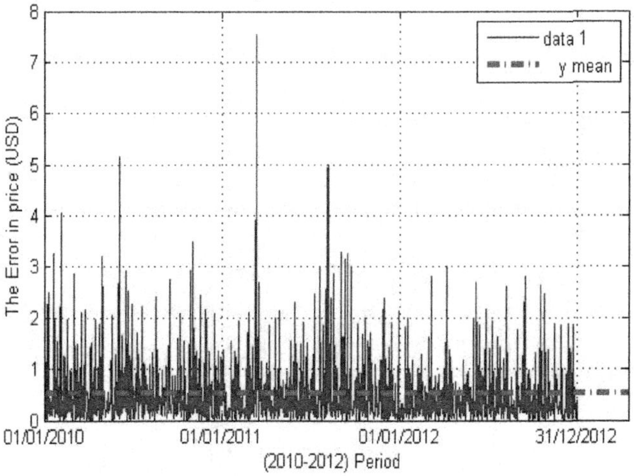


Figure 5.8: The closing price absolute prediction error in TK stock mark

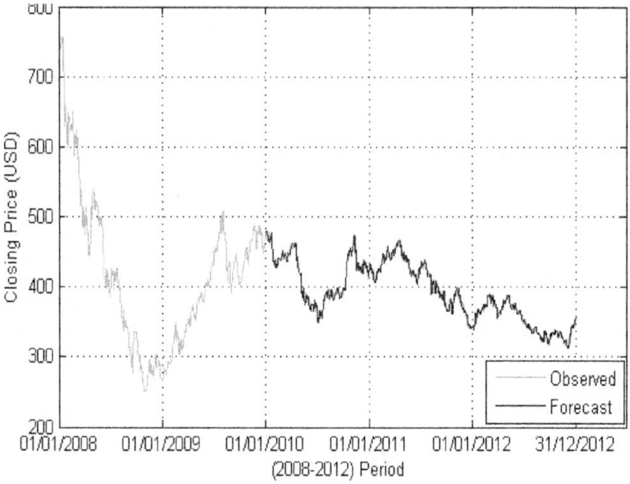


Figure 5.9: ARMA (9, 10) closing and forecasting price for 3 years in SH

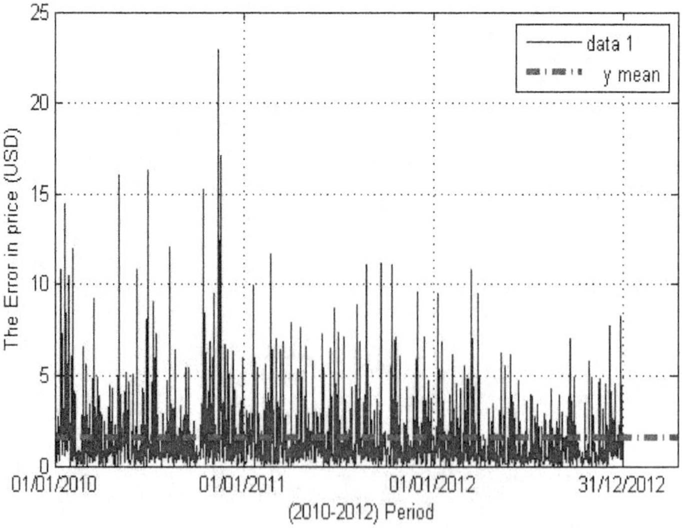


Figure 5.10: The closing price absolute prediction error in SH stock market

Table 5.3 contain sample of the Actual and prediction values by ARMA in all these stock markets.

Table 5.3: Actual and forecasting closing price

| London stock market | | |
|---|---|---|
| Date | Actual price | ARMA forecasting |
| 01/01/2010 | 8686.322 | 8789.0537 |
| 02/01/2010 | 8752.0595 | 8874.3535 |
| 03/01/2010 | 8817.797 | 8909.1603 |
| 04/01/2010 | 8883.5345 | 8934.1211 |
| 05/01/2010 | 8906.688 | 8943.095 |
| 06/01/2010 | 8879.521 | 8984.8868 |
| 07/01/2010 | 8837.7459 | 8811.6198 |
| 08/01/2010 | 8834.7968 | 8778.8938 |
| 09/01/2010 | 8847.2099 | 8894.0669 |
| 10/01/2010 | 8859.623 | 8937.9644 |
| New York stock market | | |
| Date | Actual price | ARMA forecasting |
| 01/01/2010 | 1119.5725 | 1125.2987 |
| 02/01/2010 | 1124.045 | 1132.7034 |
| 03/01/2010 | 1128.5175 | 1138.759 |
| 04/01/2010 | 1132.99 | 1150.9653 |
| 05/01/2010 | 1136.52 | 1146.3868 |
| 06/01/2010 | 1137.14 | 1157.6491 |
| 07/01/2010 | 1141.69 | 1150.1642 |
| 08/01/2010 | 1144.98 | 1161.2432 |
| 09/01/2010 | 1145.6466 | 1155.459 |
| 10/01/2010 | 1146.3133 | 1161.6652 |
| Tokyo stock market | | |
| Date | Actual price | ARMA forecasting |
| 01/01/2010 | 115.7897 | 115.7822 |
| 02/01/2010 | 115.4686 | 115.5897 |
| 03/01/2010 | 115.1476 | 115.1093 |
| 04/01/2010 | 114.8265 | 115.218 |
| 05/01/2010 | 115.3619 | 115.4228 |
| 06/01/2010 | 117.7016 | 115.4295 |
| 07/01/2010 | 118.5826 | 118.5984 |
| 08/01/2010 | 115.9383 | 118.4435 |
| 09/01/2010 | 116.4044 | 116.2426 |
| 10/01/2010 | 116.8706 | 116.0371 |

| Shanghai stock market | | |
|---|---|---|
| Date | Actual price | ARMA forecasting |
| 01/01/2010 | 478.3058 | 478.7511 |
| 02/01/2010 | 477.166 | 478.2803 |
| 03/01/2010 | 476.0262 | 475.7647 |
| 04/01/2010 | 474.8864 | 475.2196 |
| 05/01/2010 | 480.1829 | 479.1875 |
| 06/01/2010 | 476.0923 | 478.7534 |
| 07/01/2010 | 466.7844 | 466.1087 |
| 08/01/2010 | 467.2552 | 465.0677 |
| 09/01/2010 | 468.2856 | 468.0196 |

The investment and other idea will refer to it in the next Chapter.

# Chapter 6

# THE INVESTMENT

## 6.1 Investment in Economic

In economics, Investment is complex in abounding areas, such as business administration and accounts whether for households, companies, or governments. In finance, investment is putting money into somewhat with the hesitation of gain. This may or may not be backed by analysis. Most or all forms of investment absorb some structure of risk, such as investment in stock and property. In adverse putting money into somewhat with an achievement of concise gain, with or after absolute analysis, is banking or assumption. Under the capable market hypothesis, all investments with according accident should accept the accepted amount of return but that does not anticipate one from advance in unreliable assets in the achievement of benefiting from this trade-off [42].

## 6.2 Investment of Money among Stock Markets

The stock markets have absolutely correlation with the corporate investment, both of them depends on the time series. Keynes (1936) argues that stock prices contain an important element of irrationality [43]. This attempt is based on the values that have been predicted by ARMA($r,m$) model during 3 years (2010, 2011 and 2012). The objective of investment process between the stock markets (New York, London, Tokyo, and Shanghai) is to find out which stock market is better for investment. Firstly, $100 is invested in each stock market separately seeking to calculate the value of investment at the end of 3 years. Figure 6.1 shows the steps of investment in each stock market.

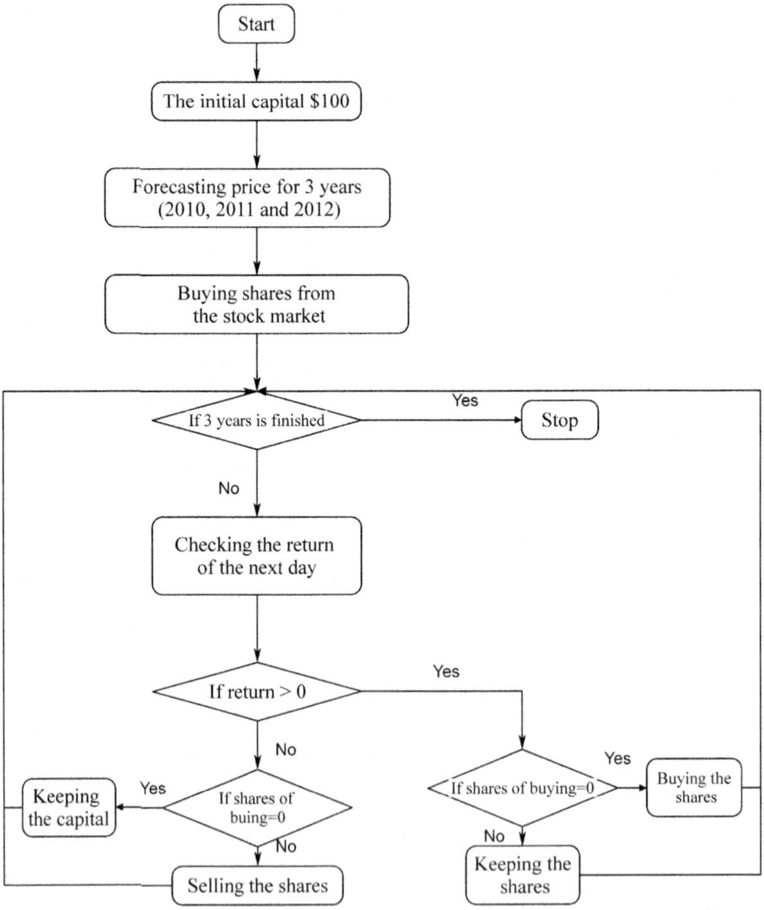


Figure 6.1: Block diagram of investment in each stock market

Secondly, testing the outcomes of the investment process in the abovementioned stock markets to identify the value of investment in the same period. In each stock market the value of the return determines the decision of buying or selling in the day. In the process of investment among the stock markets, shares are purchased from and sold in the best stock market which has the highest return daily during 3 years. The transfer of the invested money from one global market to another one takes one day due to banking operations. Figure 6.2 shows the steps of investment in all stock markets at the same time.

Table 6.1 to Table 6.4 contains sample of investment date, price, shares, and return value of investment for each stock market, for example in NY stock market on 05/01/2010 the prediction price ( NY p p =$1146.387), the return (NY p r= 0.0097), number of bought shares (shrb=0.087) with initial amount $100, in the next day (06/01/2010), the prediction price was $1157.649, as the return value was less than zero ( -0.0064) ,it is recommended to sell the shares, so the shares are sold with $100.9824. One day later, the capital increased by one dollar approximately. On 20/12/2011 the prediction price was $1246.005, the return was 0.0061, number of bought shares was 1.292 with amount $1611.067, in the next day (21/12/2011) the prediction price was $1253.694, as the return value was more than zero (0.0067). It is recommended to keep the shares rather than selling them. See appendix E.4.

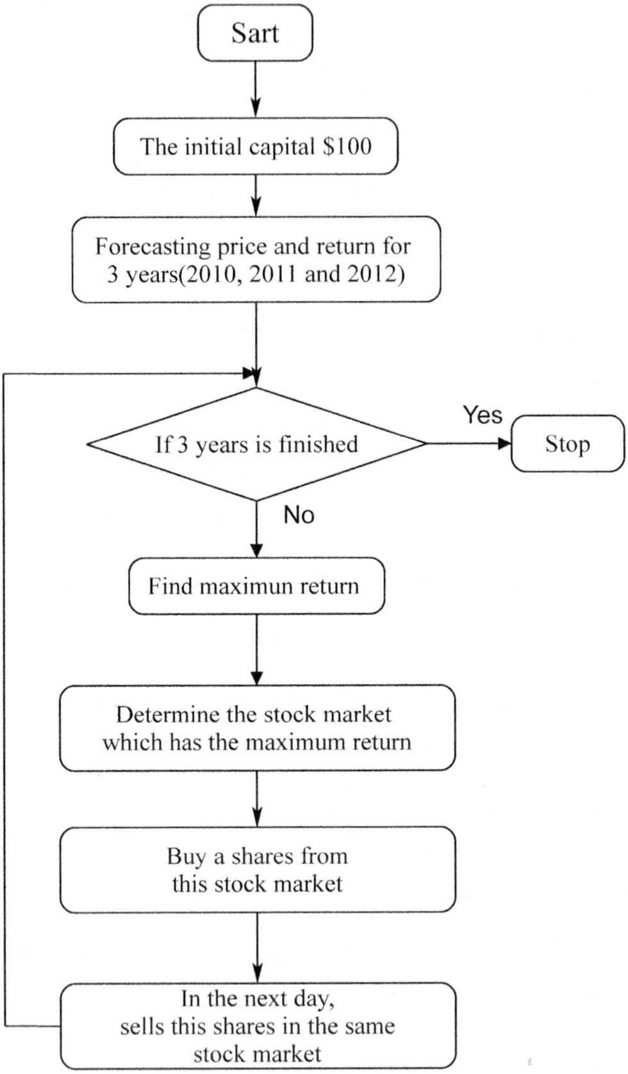


Figure 6.2: Block diagram of investment in all stock markets at the same time

Table 6.1: Investment date, stock market, and value in NYSE

| Date | NY A p | NY p p | NYp r | Shr b | Shr s | Invp b | Invp s |
|---|---|---|---|---|---|---|---|
| 05/01/2010 | 1136.52 | 1146.387 | 0.0097 | 0.087 | 0 | 100 | 0 |
| 06/01/2010 | 1137.14 | 1157.649 | -0.0064 | 0 | 0.0872 | 0 | 100.9824 |
| 07/01/2010 | 1141.69 | 1150.164 | 0.0095 | 0.087 | 0 | 100.982 | 0 |
| 08/01/2010 | 1144.98 | 1161.243 | -0.0049 | 0 | 0.0878 | 0 | 101.9551 |
| 09/01/2010 | 1146.98 | 1155.459 | 0.0054 | 0.088 | 0 | 101.9551 | 0 |
| 12/01/2010 | 1136.22 | 1156.94 | -0.0044 | 0 | 0.0882 | 0 | 102.0857 |
| 13/01/2010 | 1145.68 | 1151.909 | 0.0065 | 0.088 | 0 | 102.0857 | 0 |
| 14/01/2010 | 1148.46 | 1159.461 | -0.0156 | 0 | 0.0886 | 0 | 102.7551 |
| 15/01/2010 | 1136.03 | 1141.503 | 0.005 | 0.09 | 0 | 102.7551 | 0 |
| 16/01/2010 | 1150.23 | 1147.245 | 0.0015 | 0.09 | 0 | 102.7551 | 0 |
| 2011 | | | | | | | |
| Date | NY A p | NY p p | NYp r | Shr b | Shr s | Invp b | Invp s |
| 16/12/2011 | 1205.35 | 1224.848 | 0.0034 | 1.3107 | 0 | 1575.367 | 0 |
| 17/12/2011 | 1241.3 | 1229.093 | -0.0255 | 0 | 1.3107 | 0 | 1611.067 |
| 20/12/2011 | 1243.72 | 1246.005 | 0.0061 | 1.292 | 0 | 1611.067 | 0 |
| 21/12/2011 | 1254 | 1253.694 | 0.0067 | 1.292 | 0 | 1611.067 | 0 |
| 22/12/2011 | 1265.33 | 1262.206 | 0.002 | 1.292 | 0 | 1611.067 | 0 |
| 23/12/2011 | 1265.43 | 1264.766 | -0.0011 | 0 | 1.292 | 0 | 1635.324 |
| 24/12/2011 | 1249.64 | 1263.319 | -0.0012 | 0 | 1.292 | 0 | 1635.324 |
| 29/12/2011 | 1263.02 | 1222.403 | 0.024 | 1.337 | 0 | 1635.324 | 0 |
| 30/12/2011 | 1257.6 | 1252.172 | -0.005 | 0 | 1.337 | 0 | 1675.148 |
| 2012 | | | | | | | |
| Date | NY A p | NY p p | NYp r | Shr b | Shr s | Invp b | Invp s |
| 14/12/2012 | 1435.81 | 1394.778 | -0.0156 | 0 | 6.6662 | 0 | 9431.54 |
| 15/12/2012 | 1443.69 | 1373.165 | 0.0259 | 6.8684 | 0 | 9431.54 | 0 |
| 18/12/2012 | 1430.15 | 1433.655 | -0.0142 | 0 | 6.8685 | 0 | 9847.0119 |
| 19/12/2012 | 1426.66 | 1413.4 | 0.0084 | 6.9669 | 0 | 9847.0118 | 0 |
| 20/12/2012 | 1419.83 | 1425.326 | -0.0149 | 0 | 6.9669 | 0 | 9930.1008 |
| 21/12/2012 | 1418.1 | 1404.207 | 0.0082 | 7.0717 | 0 | 9930.1008 | 0 |
| 22/12/2012 | 1402.43 | 1415.769 | -0.0142 | 0 | 7.0717 | 0 | 10011.8619 |
| 25/12/2012 | 1426.19 | 1386.916 | 0.0066 | 7.2188 | 0 | 10011.8619 | 0 |
| 28/12/2012 | 1402.43 | 1382.087 | -0.017 | 0 | 7.2187 | 0 | 9977.0023 |

Table 6.2: Investment date, stock market, and value in LSE

| Date | LD A p | LD p p | LD p r | Shr b | Shr s | Invp b | Ivnp s |
|---|---|---|---|---|---|---|---|
| 05/01/2010 | 8906.688 | 8943.095 | 0.0047 | 0.0112 | 0 | 100 | 0 |
| 06/01/2010 | 8879.521 | 8984.887 | -0.01947 | 0 | 0.0112 | 0 | 100.4673 |
| 07/01/2010 | 8837.74597 | 8811.62 | -0.0037 | 0 | 0.0112 | 0 | 100.4673 |
| 08/01/2010 | 8834.79688 | 8778.894 | 0.013 | 0.0114 | 0 | 100.467 | 0 |
| 09/01/2010 | 8872.0362 | 8894.067 | 0.0049 | 0.0114 | 0 | 100.467 | 0 |
| 12/01/2010 | 8860.60518 | 8917.91 | -0.0083 | 0 | 0.0114 | 0 | 102.05824 |
| 13/01/2010 | 8825.4714 | 8843.481 | 0.0029 | 0.0115 | 0 | 102.0582 | 0 |
| 14/01/2010 | 8919.72986 | 8869.615 | 0.0039 | 0.0115 | 0 | 102.0582 | 0 |
| 15/01/2010 | 8889.5743 | 8904.704 | 0.0012 | 0.0115 | 0 | 102.0582 | 0 |
| 16/01/2010 | 8932.24608 | 8915.027 | -0.0002 | 0 | 0.0115 | 0 | 102.8839 |
| 2011 | | | | | | | |
| Date | LD A p | LD p p | LD p r | Shr b | Shr s | Invp b | Ivnp s |
| 16/12/2011 | 8340.61786 | 8306.523 | 0.0163 | 0.5476 | 0 | 4548.6162 | 0 |
| 17/12/2011 | 8336.6735 | 8442.906 | -0.0016 | 0 | 0.5475 | 0 | 4623.2991 |
| 20/12/2011 | 8404.17372 | 8458.106 | 0.0208 | 0.5466 | 0 | 4623.2991 | 0 |
| 21/12/2011 | 8399.30848 | 8636.226 | 0.0012 | 0.5466 | 0 | 4623.2991 | 0 |
| 22/12/2011 | 8558.7588 | 8646.05 | 0.0142 | 0.5466 | 0 | 4623.2991 | 0 |
| 23/12/2011 | 8641.70852 | 8769.677 | -0.0141 | 0 | 0.5466 | 0 | 4793.6072 |
| 24/12/2011 | 8615.22582 | 8646.901 | 0.005 | 0.5543 | 0 | 4793.6072 | 0 |
| 29/12/2011 | 8690.88816 | 8706.916 | -0.0105 | 0 | 0.5543 | 0 | 4826.8777 |
| 30/12/2011 | 8595.82998 | 8616.435 | 0.005 | 0.5602 | 0 | 4826.8777 | 0 |
| 2012 | | | | | | | |
| Date | LD A p | LD p p | LD p r | Shr b | Shr s | Invp b | Ivnp s |
| 14/12/2012 | 9551.27122 | 9502.816 | -0.00976 | 0 | 1.9894 | 0 | 19013.0782 |
| 15/12/2012 | 9561.04812 | 9410.549 | 0.0121 | 2.0204 | 0 | 19013.0781 | 0 |
| 18/12/2012 | 9607.84774 | 9586.822 | -0.0089 | 0 | 2.0204 | 0 | 19369.220 |
| 19/12/2012 | 9669.11904 | 9501.744 | 0.0194 | 2.0385 | 0 | 19369.22 | 0 |
| 20/12/2012 | 9692.96244 | 9688.506 | -0.008 | 0 | 2.0384 | 0 | 19749.9325 |
| 21/12/2012 | 9659.034 | 9611.312 | -0.0046 | 0 | 2.0384 | 0 | 19749.9325 |
| 22/12/2012 | 9625.55972 | 9566.505 | -0.0114 | 0 | 2.0384 | 0 | 19749.9325 |
| 25/12/2012 | 9604.88133 | 9505.303 | 0.0039 | 2.0778 | 0 | 19749.9325 | 0 |
| 28/12/2012 | 9561.81798 | 9519.222 | -0.0096 | 0 | 2.0777 | 0 | 19778.8538 |

Table 6.3: Investment date, stock market, and value in TSE

| Date | TK A p | TK p p | TK p r | Shr b | Shr s | Invp b | Invp s |
|---|---|---|---|---|---|---|---|
| 05/01/2010 | 114.8265 | 115.4228 | 0.00005 | 0.8664 | 0 | 100 | 0 |
| 06/01/2010 | 115.3619 | 115.4295 | 0.027083 | 0.8664 | 0 | 100 | 0 |
| 07/01/2010 | 117.7017 | 118.5984 | -0.00131 | 0 | 0.8664 | 0 | 102.7513 |
| 08/01/2010 | 118.5826 | 118.4436 | -0.01876 | 0 | 0.8664 | 0 | 102.7513 |
| 09/01/2010 | 115.9383 | 116.2426 | -0.00177 | 0 | 0.8664 | 0 | 102.7513 |
| 12/01/2010 | 117.8029 | 117.5399 | 0.017045 | 0.8742 | 0 | 102.7513 | 0 |
| 13/01/2010 | 119.7049 | 119.5605 | -0.00238 | 0 | 0.8742 | 0 | 104.5177 |
| 14/01/2010 | 119.4059 | 119.2765 | -0.01802 | 0 | 0.8742 | 0 | 104.5177 |
| 15/01/2010 | 117.3374 | 117.1463 | -0.00083 | 0 | 0.8742 | 0 | 104.5177 |
| 16/01/2010 | 118.1127 | 115.4228 | 0.006059 | 0.8929 | 0 | 104.5177 | 0 |
| 2011 | | | | | | | |
| Date | TK A p | TK p p | TK p r | Shr b | Shr s | Invp b | Invp s |
| 16/12/2011 | 108.9187 | 106.927 | 0.003805 | 6.4033 | 0 | 684.6869 | 0 |
| 17/12/2011 | 110.0632 | 107.3346 | 0.005748 | 0 | 6.4033 | 0 | 687.4528 |
| 20/12/2011 | 111.1575 | 107.359 | -0.00029 | 6.4052 | 0 | 687.4528 | 0 |
| 21/12/2011 | 112.3158 | 107.3277 | 0.005377 | 0 | 6.4052 | 0 | 691.1591 |
| 22/12/2011 | 113.9627 | 107.9063 | -0.00088 | 0 | 6.4052 | 0 | 691.1591 |
| 23/12/2011 | 113.9567 | 107.8112 | -0.00046 | 6.41377 | 0 | 691.1591 | 0 |
| 24/12/2011 | 114.2093 | 107.7618 | 3.97E-05 | 6.41377 | 0 | 691.1591 | 0 |
| 29/12/2011 | 115.488 | 108.2896 | 0.010864 | 0 | 6.4138 | 0 | 702.1314 |
| 30/12/2011 | 115.0431 | 109.4725 | -0.00158 | 0 | 6.4138 | 0 | 702.1314 |
| 2012 | | | | | | | |
| Date | TK A p | TK p p | TK p r | Shr b | Shr s | Invp b | Invp s |
| 14/12/2012 | 121.8112 | 119.0257 | -0.00293 | 0 | 13.3411 | 0 | 1587.9374 |
| 15/12/2012 | 122.6631 | 118.6773 | 0.018016 | 13.3803 | 0 | 1587.9374 | 0 |
| 18/12/2012 | 122.6631 | 119.1056 | -0.00183 | 0 | 13.3803 | 0 | 1593.6682 |
| 19/12/2012 | 121.9248 | 118.8875 | 0.008488 | 13.4048 | 0 | 1593.6681 | 0 |
| 20/12/2012 | 119.468 | 119.9009 | -7.28E-05 | 0 | 13.4048 | 0 | 1607.2526 |
| 21/12/2012 | 118.2867 | 119.8922 | 0.016871 | 13.4058 | 0 | 1607.2526 | 0 |
| 22/12/2012 | 121.7413 | 121.9321 | -0.00095 | 0 | 13.4058 | 0 | 1634.5985 |
| 25/12/2012 | 121.8112 | 121.1701 | 0.012903 | 13.4901 | 0 | 1634.5986 | 0 |
| 28/12/2012 | 122.6631 | 122.4198 | -0.00122 | 0 | 13.4901 | 0 | 1651.457 |

Table 6.4: Investment date, stock market, and value in SSE

| Date | SH A p | SH p p | SH p r | Shr b | Shr s | Invp b | Invp s |
|---|---|---|---|---|---|---|---|
| 05/01/2010 | 474.886464 | 479.1875 | -0.00091 | 0.2086 | 0 | 100 | 0 |
| 06/01/2010 | 480.182934 | 478.7534 | -0.02677 | 0 | 0.2087 | 0 | 99.9094 |
| 07/01/2010 | 476.092386 | 466.1087 | -0.00224 | 0 | 0.2087 | 0 | 99.9094 |
| 08/01/2010 | 466.784436 | 465.0677 | 0.006327 | 0.2148 | 0 | 99.9094 | 0 |
| 09/01/2010 | 467.2552 | 468.0197 | -0.00169 | 0 | 0.2148 | 0 | 100.5436 |
| 12/01/2010 | 476.092386 | 468.1921 | -0.00716 | 0 | 0.2148 | 0 | 100.5436 |
| 13/01/2010 | 480.182934 | 464.852 | -0.00363 | 0 | 0.2148 | 0 | 100.5436 |
| 14/01/2010 | 476.092386 | 463.1671 | 0.016362 | 0.2171 | 0 | 100.5436 | 0 |
| 15/01/2010 | 466.784436 | 470.8079 | -0.00061 | 0 | 0.2171 | 0 | 102.2022 |
| 16/01/2010 | 467.2552 | 470.5205 | 0.003231 | 0.2172 | 0 | 102.2022 | 0 |
| 2011 | | | | | | | |
| Date | SH A p | SH p p | SH p r | Shr b | Shr s | Invp b | Invp s |
| 16/12/2011 | 366.083787 | 346.5929 | 0.000213 | 1.4576 | 0 | 505.1772 | 0 |
| 17/12/2011 | 365.865643 | 346.6666 | -0.00054 | 0 | 1.45755 | 0 | 505.2845 |
| 20/12/2011 | 367.404975 | 347.7359 | 0.001086 | 1.4531 | 0 | 505.2845 | 0 |
| 21/12/2011 | 366.94665 | 348.1138 | -0.01625 | 0 | 1.45307 | 0 | 505.8337 |
| 22/12/2011 | 364.655025 | 342.502 | -0.00157 | 0 | 1.45307 | 0 | 505.8337 |
| 23/12/2011 | 359.77178 | 341.9637 | 0.011464 | 1.4792 | 0 | 505.8337 | 0 |
| 24/12/2011 | 352.129194 | 345.9065 | 0.000213 | 1.4792 | 0 | 505.8337 | 0 |
| 29/12/2011 | 348.540528 | 341.0527 | 0.012587 | 1.4792 | 0 | 505.8337 | 0 |
| 30/12/2011 | 340.65658 | 345.3725 | 0.001814 | 1.4792 | 0 | 505.8337 | 0 |
| 2012 | | | | | | | |
| Date | SH A p | SH p p | SH p r | Shr b | Shr s | Invp b | Invp s |
| 14/12/2012 | 343.579936 | 342.574 | 0.004845 | 2.8113 | 0 | 886.2499 | 0 |
| 15/12/2012 | 344.76765 | 344.2379 | -0.00238 | 0 | 2.8113 | 0 | 967.7702 |
| 18/12/2012 | 341.945628 | 344.6355 | 0.002026 | 2.8081 | 0 | 967.7702 | 0 |
| 19/12/2012 | 341.99352 | 345.3343 | -0.0031 | 0 | 2.8081 | 0 | 969.7325 |
| 20/12/2012 | 350.857185 | 344.2669 | -0.00015 | 0 | 2.8081 | 0 | 969.7325 |
| 21/12/2012 | 351.732105 | 344.2163 | -0.00362 | 0 | 2.8081 | 0 | 969.7325 |
| 22/12/2012 | 349.63515 | 342.9717 | 1.54E-03 | 2.8274 | 0 | 969.7325 | 0 |
| 25/12/2012 | 353.523475 | 342.5775 | 0.028793 | 2.8274 | 0 | 969.7325 | 0 |
| 28/12/2012 | 353.523475 | 353.9074 | 0.002493 | 2.8274 0 | 0 | 969.7325 | 0 |

Tables from 6.5 to 6.7 show the investment among the stock market at the same time, for example on 19/01/2010 the best return value was in NY stock market (NY r=0.008777), the prediction price was (NY p p= 1156.966), the amount of money was (invp b= 103.272), and number of bought shares was (shr b =0.089261). In the next day (20/01/2010) the shares sold in the said market (shr s=0.089261), therefore, the capital became 104.5944 (it increased by 1.2184 approximately). See appendix D.

On 21/01/2010, the best return value was in TK stock market (0.001926), the prediction price was 115.3501, and the invested amount was 104.1824, the number of shares bought from this stock market was (shr b= 0.903184). On 22/01/2010, the amount of money obtained from the sale of shares in TK stock market was (invp s =104.3833), so it increased by $0.2. Additionally, on 23/01/2010, the best return value was in LD stock market (LD r=0.011975), the prediction price was (LD p p= 8572.58), the amount of money was (invp b= 104.3833), and the number of bought shares was (shr b= 0.012176). On 26/01/2010, the amount of money that was gained due to the sold the shares in LD stock market was (invp s =103.3762). So, it decreased by (-$1.0071). The best return was in LD stock market on 27/01/2010. One day later, on 28/01/2010, (shr s=0.012107) shares were sold in LD stock market for (invp s =$104.5944), so there was an increase by $1.2182. See appendix E.4.

Regarding the transactions in each stock market as mentioned in Table 6.8, the number of transactions is calculated based on the frequency of sales transactions in each stock market.

Table 6.5: Investment date, stock market, and value in 2010

| Date | LD A p | NY A p | SH AP | TK A p | LD p p | NY p p | SH p p | TK p p | LD r | NY r | SH r | TK r | M b | M s | Shr b | Shr s | Invp b | Invp s |
|---|---|---|---|---|---|---|---|---|---|---|---|---|---|---|---|---|---|---|
| 05/01/2010 | 8906.688 | 1136.52 | 474.8864 | 114.8265 | 8943.095 | 1146.387 | 479.1875 | 115.4228 | 0.004662 | 0.0097 | -0.00091 | 5.82E-05 | NY | | 0.087231 | 0 | 100 | 0 |
| 06/01/2010 | 8879.521 | 1137.14 | 480.1829 | 115.3619 | 8984.887 | 1157.649 | 478.7534 | 115.4295 | -0.01947 | -0.00649 | -0.02677 | 0.027083 | | NY | 0 | 0.087231 | 0 | 100.9824 |
| 07/01/2010 | 8837.74597 | 1141.69 | 476.0923 | 117.7017 | 8811.62 | 1150.164 | 466.1087 | 118.5984 | -0.00372 | 0.009586 | -0.00224 | -0.00131 | NY | | 0.087798 | 0 | 100.9824 | 0 |
| 08/01/2010 | 8834.79688 | 1144.98 | 466.7844 | 118.5826 | 8778.894 | 1161.243 | 465.0677 | 118.4436 | 0.013034 | -0.00499 | 0.006327 | -0.01876 | | NY | 0 | 0.087798 | 0 | 101.9551 |
| 09/01/2010 | 8872.0362 | 1146.98 | 467.2552 | 115.9383 | 8894.067 | 1155.459 | 468.0197 | 116.2426 | 0.004923 | 0.005357 | -0.00169 | -0.00177 | NY | | 0.088238 | 0 | 101.9551 | 0 |
| 12/01/2010 | 8860.60518 | 1136.22 | 476.0923 | 117.8029 | 8917.91 | 1156.94 | 468.1921 | 117.5399 | -0.00838 | -0.00436 | -0.00716 | 0.017045 | | NY | 0 | 0.088238 | 0 | 102.0858 |
| 13/01/2010 | 8825.4714 | 1145.68 | 480.1829 | 119.7049 | 8843.481 | 1151.909 | 464.852 | 119.5605 | 0.002951 | 0.006535 | -0.00363 | -0.00238 | NY | | 0.088623 | 0 | 102.0858 | 0 |
| 14/01/2010 | 8919.72986 | 1148.46 | 476.0923 | 119.4059 | 8869.615 | 1159.461 | 463.1671 | 119.2765 | 0.003948 | -0.01561 | 0.016362 | -0.01802 | | NY | 0 | 0.088623 | 0 | 102.7551 |
| 15/01/2010 | 8889.5743 | 1136.03 | 466.7844 | 117.3374 | 8904.704 | 1141.503 | 470.8079 | 117.1463 | 0.001159 | 0.005018 | -0.00061 | -0.00083 | NY | | 0.090017 | 0 | 102.7551 | 0 |
| 16/01/2010 | 8932.24608 | 1150.23 | 467.2552 | 118.1127 | 8915.027 | 1147.245 | 470.5205 | 117.0495 | -0.00017 | 0.00153 | 0.003231 | 0.006059 | | NY | 0 | 0.090017 | 0 | 103.272 |
| 19/01/2010 | 8992.41741 | 1138.04 | 470.3466 | 119.5525 | 9060.534 | 1156.966 | 475.6205 | 119.7989 | 0.00397 | 0.008777 | -0.00018 | -0.00034 | NY | | 0.089261 | 0 | 103.272 | 0 |
| 20/01/2010 | 8878.72832 | 1116.48 | 478.9818 | 116.4961 | 9096.572 | 1167.165 | 475.5363 | 119.7582 | -0.05915 | -0.04275 | -0.03429 | -0.0375 | | NY | 0 | 0.089261 | 0 | 104.1824 |
| 21/01/2010 | 8696.74651 | 1091.76 | 464.1601 | 115.6396 | 8574.087 | 1118.32 | 459.5071 | 115.3501 | -0.0075 | -0.00029 | -0.00106 | 0.001926 | TK | | 0.903184 | 0 | 104.1824 | 0 |
| 22/01/2010 | 8605.7084 | 1096.78 | 470.4349 | 113.5781 | 8509.995 | 1117.999 | 459.0213 | 115.5725 | 0.007327 | -0.01618 | -0.00878 | -0.01736 | | TK | 0 | 0.903184 | 0 | 104.3833 |
| 23/01/2010 | 8472.76521 | 1092.17 | 471.6931 | 113.7981 | 8572.58 | 1100.06 | 455.0099 | 113.5833 | 0.011975 | 0.009336 | -0.00342 | 0.005569 | LD | | 0.012176 | 0 | 104.3833 | 0 |
| 26/01/2010 | 8523.77657 | 1097.5 | 474.2351 | 115.5986 | 8489.874 | 1114.2 | 452.2312 | 114.0694 | 0.005727 | -0.00957 | -0.03776 | -0.00646 | | LD | 0 | 0.012176 | 0 | 103.3762 |
| 27/01/2010 | 8445.56725 | 1084.53 | 475.0171 | 113.1982 | 8538.638 | 1103.593 | 435.4727 | 113.3344 | 0.011715 | 0.010036 | -0.00399 | -0.00139 | LD | | 0.012107 | 0 | 103.3762 | 0 |
| 28/01/2010 | 8317.5094 | 1073.87 | 461.1156 | 114.2962 | 8639.258 | 1114.724 | 433.7396 | 113.177 | -0.02365 | -0.02736 | 0.006883 | 0.019178 | | LD | 0 | 0.012107 | 0 | 104.5944 |
| 29/01/2010 | 8401.2192 | 1089.19 | 462.1412 | 115.1191 | 8437.344 | 1084.639 | 436.7353 | 115.3684 | 0.0109 | 0.0183 | -0.0034 | -0.0025 | NY | | 0.0964 | 0 | 104.5944 | 0 |
| 30/01/2010 | 8384.29572 | 1103.32 | 457.399858 | 115.4881 | 8530.002 | 1104.674 | 435.2398 | 115.0784 | -0.00456 | -0.00445 | -0.0077 | 0.003493 | | NY | 0 | 0.0964 | 0 | 106.5264 |
| 02/02/2010 | 8418.41022 | 1097.28 | 453.021624 | 114.9514 | 8431.515 | 1116.023 | 429.0406 | 114.5555 | 0.014451 | 0.012 | -0.00353 | 0.001037 | LD | | 0.012634 | 0 | 106.5264 | 0 |
| 03/02/2010 | 8378.6945 | 1063.11 | 441.736757 | 110.628 | 8554.24 | 1129.496 | 427.5274 | 114.6744 | -0.03958 | -0.05863 | 0.023883 | -0.04732 | | LD | 0 | 0.012634 | 0 | 108.077 |
| 04/02/2010 | 8209.51782 | 1066.19 | 436.941043 | 109.47 | 8222.277 | 1065.177 | 437.8608 | 109.3743 | -0.00289 | 0.004463 | -0.0011 | 0.00328 | NY | | 0.101464 | 0 | 108.077 | 0 |
| 05/02/2010 | 8023.04477 | 1056.74 | 438.042682 | 109.2619 | 8198.511 | 1069.941 | 437.3792 | 109.7336 | -0.01741 | 0.00425 | -0.01939 | 0.005729 | | NY | 0 | 0.101464 | 0 | 108.5604 |
| 06/02/2010 | 7973.01411 | 1070.52 | 437.333127 | 111.5967 | 8057.006 | 1074.498 | 428.9815 | 110.3641 | 0.019041 | 0.015488 | 0.00034 | 0.004965 | LD | | 0.013474 | 0 | 108.5604 | 0 |

Table 6.6: Investment date, stock market, and value in 2011

| Date | LD A p | NY A p | SH AP | TK A p | LD p p | NY p p | SH p p | TK p p | LND r | NY r | SH r | TK r | M b | M s | Shr b | Shr s | Invp b | Invp s |
|---|---|---|---|---|---|---|---|---|---|---|---|---|---|---|---|---|---|---|
| 05/01/2011 | 9394.03377 | 1276.56 | 433.482252 | 127.7409 | 9270.778 | 1263.862 | 431.9564 | 129.1168 | 0.008319 | 0.004817 | -0.0127 | -0.01767 | | LD | 0 | 0.085201 | 0 | 789.8798 |
| 06/01/2011 | 9360.3225 | 1273.85 | 427.938 | 126.2915 | 9348.22 | 1269.966 | 426.506 | 126.8552 | -0.00432 | -0.00314 | -0.00098 | -0.00126 | SH | | 1.851978 | 0 | 789.8798 | 0 |
| 07/01/2011 | 9275.665 | 1271.5 | 434.454856 | 124.3217 | 9307.884 | 1265.983 | 426.0864 | 126.6953 | -0.01335 | 0.000332 | 0.000123 | -0.00312 | | SH | 0 | 1.851978 | 0 | 789.1028 |
| 08/01/2011 | 9255.49457 | 1269.75 | 431.685 | 126.2103 | 9184.428 | 1266.403 | 426.1389 | 126.3003 | -0.00672 | -0.00514 | -0.00103 | 0.001982 | TK | | 6.24783 | 0 | 789.1028 | 0 |
| 11/01/2011 | 9345.756 | 1274.48 | 428.854044 | 126.6195 | 9242.453 | 1256.373 | 419.1231 | 126.8823 | 0.020307 | 0.02215 | 0.015934 | -0.00815 | | TK | 0 | 6.24783 | 0 | 792.7391 |
| 12/01/2011 | 9422.15004 | 1285.96 | 425.841032 | 125.863 | 9432.055 | 1284.513 | 425.8551 | 125.8525 | 0.001196 | -0.00331 | -0.00074 | -0.00045 | LD | | 0.084047 | 0 | 792.7391 | 0 |
| 13/01/2011 | 9429.81306 | 1283.76 | 419.71326 | 126.7918 | 9443.346 | 1280.263 | 425.542 | 125.7955 | 0.002333 | 0.007885 | -0.00923 | 0.012127 | | LD | 0 | 0.084047 | 0 | 793.6881 |
| 14/01/2011 | 9472.51422 | 1293.24 | 411.588294 | 125.3601 | 9465.402 | 1290.398 | 421.6328 | 127.3303 | -0.00767 | -0.00307 | -0.00109 | -0.00103 | TK | | 6.233299 | 0 | 793.6881 | 0 |
| 15/01/2011 | 9495.71448 | 1295.02 | 414.655571 | 124.9026 | 9393.113 | 1286.445 | 421.1728 | 127.1991 | 0.006608 | 0.003704 | -0.01683 | 0.002446 | | TK | 0 | 6.233299 | 0 | 792.8701 |
| 18/01/2011 | 9615.14064 | 1281.92 | 416.143156 | 124.3215 | 9603.71 | 1290.551 | 409.0298 | 125.9447 | -0.00269 | -0.0047 | -0.002 | -0.00075 | TK | | 6.295382 | 0 | 792.8701 | 0 |
| 19/01/2011 | 9535.82485 | 1280.26 | 424.581696 | 127.5798 | 9577.892 | 1284.497 | 408.2143 | 125.8498 | -0.03453 | -0.01156 | -0.00426 | 0.003159 | | TK | 0 | 6.295382 | 0 | 792.2727 |
| 20/01/2011 | 9383.94568 | 1283.35 | 424.581696 | 127.2626 | 9252.826 | 1269.732 | 406.4797 | 126.248 | -0.01762 | -0.0086 | -0.00195 | 0.000526 | TK | | 6.275525 | 0 | 792.2727 | 0 |
| 21/01/2011 | 9399.88146 | 1290.84 | 432.176475 | 128.6309 | 9091.233 | 1258.86 | 405.6863 | 126.3144 | 0.039247 | 0.017386 | 0.012858 | 0.000382 | | TK | 0 | 6.275525 | 0 | 792.6893 |
| 22/01/2011 | 9506.07927 | 1291.18 | 428.910949 | 130.2821 | 9455.13 | 1280.938 | 410.9362 | 126.3626 | 0.004121 | -0.00725 | 0.000297 | 0.000651 | LD | | 0.083837 | 0 | 792.6893 | 0 |
| 25/01/2011 | 9451.75044 | 1296.63 | 427.58388 | 129.759 | 9356.698 | 1280.113 | 407.3242 | 125.4463 | 0.013948 | 0.00977 | 0.009549 | -0.00028 | | LD | 0 | 0.083837 | 0 | 784.4372 |
| 26/01/2011 | 9485.65572 | 1299.54 | 427.80716 | 129.5375 | 9488.123 | 1292.682 | 411.2322 | 125.4107 | -0.00071 | -0.00272 | 0.000958 | -0.0014 | SH | | 1.907529 | 0 | 784.4372 | 0 |
| 27/01/2011 | 9448.12189 | 1276.34 | 420.725767 | 129.3889 | 9481.401 | 1289.17 | 411.6264 | 125.2351 | -0.02368 | -0.01385 | 0.01312 | -0.00739 | | SH | 0 | 1.907529 | 0 | 785.1892 |
| 28/01/2011 | 9364.36508 | 1286.12 | 422.009525 | 130.8516 | 9259.554 | 1271.44 | 417.0624 | 124.3129 | -0.01361 | -0.00678 | -0.00017 | -0.0011 | SH | | 1.882666 | 0 | 785.1892 | 0 |
| 29/01/2011 | 9291.52392 | 1307.59 | 425.45204 | 130.0347 | 9134.409 | 1262.845 | 416.993 | 124.1764 | 0.013775 | 0.009454 | 0.012253 | 0.020174 | | SH | 0 | 1.882666 | 0 | 785.0585 |

Table 6.7: Investment date, stock market, and value in 2012

| Date | LD A p | NY A p | SH AP | TK A p | LD p p | NY p p | SH p p | TK p p | LD r | NY r | SH r | TK r | M b | M s | Shr b | Shr s | Invp b | Invp s |
|---|---|---|---|---|---|---|---|---|---|---|---|---|---|---|---|---|---|---|
| 04/12/2012 | 9422.6795 | 1418.07 | 323.055008 | 122.6631 | 9417.619 | 1391.06 | 315.241 | 116.4419 | -0.00454 | -0.01163 | 0.001608 | 6.63E-05 | | NY | 0 | 9.031513 | 0 | 12563.38 |
| 05/12/2012 | 9487.45942 | 1418.55 | 328.030789 | 122.6631 | 9374.941 | 1374.979 | 315.7484 | 116.4496 | 0.010622 | 0.017655 | 0.024731 | -0.00254 | SH | | 39.7892 | 0 | 12563.38 | 0 |
| 06/12/2012 | 9502.43428 | 1427.84 | 330.902676 | 122.6631 | 9475.056 | 1399.47 | 323.6544 | 116.1545 | -0.0059 | -0.01565 | 0.000839 | -0.00017 | | SH | 0 | 39.7892 | 0 | 12877.95 |
| 07/12/2012 | 9514.49528 | 1428.48 | 329.8773 | 121.9248 | 9419.33 | 1377.74 | 323.9259 | 116.1346 | 0.005609 | 0.017244 | 0.019394 | -0.00743 | SH | | 39.75585 | 0 | 12877.95 | 0 |
| 08/12/2012 | 9498.2464 | 1419.45 | 330.945797 | 119.468 | 9472.31 | 1401.703 | 330.2695 | 115.2751 | -0.00722 | -0.01434 | 0.0036 | 6.14E-05 | | SH | 0 | 39.75585 | 0 | 13130.14 |
| 11/12/2012 | 9507.255 | 1413.58 | 327.77532 | 118.2867 | 9381.942 | 1382.928 | 331.2747 | 116.0006 | 0.018504 | 0.022812 | 0.00062 | 0.015257 | NY | | 9.494453 | 0 | 13130.14 | 0 |
| 12/12/2012 | 9565.16933 | 1430.36 | 341.94858 | 119.9534 | 9557.164 | 1414.838 | 331.4803 | 117.784 | -0.00469 | -0.01269 | 0.00266 | -0.00225 | | NY | 0 | 9.494453 | 0 | 13433.11 |
| 13/12/2012 | 9562.07296 | 1446.79 | 343.278026 | 121.7413 | 9512.412 | 1397.002 | 332.3631 | 117.519 | -0.00101 | -0.00159 | 0.03026 | 0.012739 | SH | | 40.41699 | 0 | 13433.11 | 0 |
| 14/12/2012 | 9551.27122 | 1435.81 | 343.579936 | 121.8112 | 9502.816 | 1394.778 | 342.574 | 119.0257 | -0.00976 | -0.01562 | 0.004845 | -0.00293 | | SH | 0 | 40.41699 | 0 | 13845.81 |
| 15/12/2012 | 9561.04812 | 1443.69 | 344.76765 | 122.6631 | 9410.549 | 1373.165 | 344.2379 | 118.6773 | 0.012085 | 0.025933 | -0.00238 | 0.018016 | NY | | 10.08314 | 0 | 13845.81 | 0 |
| 18/12/2012 | 9607.84774 | 1430.15 | 341.945628 | 122.6631 | 9586.822 | 1433.655 | 344.6355 | 119.1056 | -0.00891 | -0.01423 | 0.002026 | -0.00183 | | NY | 0 | 10.08314 | 0 | 14455.74 |
| 19/12/2012 | 9669.11904 | 1426.66 | 341.99352 | 121.9248 | 9501.744 | 1413.4 | 345.3343 | 118.8875 | 0.019465 | 0.008403 | -0.0031 | 0.008488 | LD | | 1.521377 | 0 | 14455.74 | 0 |
| 20/12/2012 | 9692.96244 | 1419.83 | 350.857185 | 119.468 | 9688.506 | 1425.326 | 344.2669 | 119.9009 | -0.008 | -0.01493 | -0.00015 | -7.28E-05 | | LD | 0 | 1.521377 | 0 | 14739.87 |
| 21/12/2012 | 9659.034 | 1418.1 | 351.732105 | 118.2867 | 9611.312 | 1404.207 | 344.2163 | 119.8922 | -0.00467 | 0.0082 | -0.00362 | 0.016871 | TK | | 122.9427 | 0 | 14739.87 | 0 |
| 22/12/2012 | 9625.55972 | 1402.43 | 349.63515 | 121.7413 | 9566.505 | 1415.769 | 342.9717 | 121.9321 | -0.01149 | -0.01427 | 1.54E-03 | -0.00095 | | TK | 0 | 122.9427 | 0 | 14990.66 |
| 25/12/2012 | 9604.88133 | 1426.19 | 353.523475 | 121.8112 | 9505.303 | 1386.916 | 342.5775 | 121.1701 | 0.003981 | 0.0066 | 0.028793 | 0.012903 | SH | | 43.75844 | 0 | 14990.66 | 0 |
| 28/12/2012 | 9561.81798 | 1402.43 | 353.523475 | 122.6631 | 9519.222 | 1382.087 | 353.9074 | 122.4198 | -0.00968 | -0.01706 | 0.002493 | -0.00122 | | SH | 0 | 43.75844 | 0 | 15486.43 |
| 29/12/2012 | 9526.71634 | 1426.19 | 359.203279 | 122.6631 | 9427.537 | 1358.714 | 354.7909 | 122.2709 | 0.006158 | 0.03441 | 0.008607 | 0.002541 | NY | | 11.39786 | 0 | 15486.43 | 0 |

As a result, the capital in New York stock market increased from $100 to $9977, in London stock market the $100 became $19779, in Tokyo stock market, the invested capital increased to $1651 and, in Shanghai, it increased to $970. However, when testing the investment of $100 among these four stock markets at the same time, the initial value of investing $100 gave $15486 in return. The investment in London stock market had the highest rate of profit and the highest number of transactions in comparison with the other stock markets.

Table 6.8: Number of transaction in the stock markets

| Stock market | Number of transactions |
|---|---|
| NY | 86 |
| LD | 153 |
| TK | 68 |
| SH | 70 |

# Chapter 7

# CONCLUSIONS AND FUTURE WORK

## 7.1 Conclusions

This research has applied Auto-Regressive Moving Average (ARMA) model on the indexes of global stock market (New York, London, Tokyo and Shanghai) from 2008 to 2012 with the aim to predict the closing price and the feasibility of investment.

For each stock market, the best structural parameter set ($r$, $m$) of ARMA($r$,$m$) model is searched among 225 cases: {ARMA(1,1), ... ARMA(15,15)}. The structural parameters $r$ and $m$ which are obtained by searching the minimum RMSE case has been overlapped with the parameters determined using the autocorrelation function (ACF) and the partial autocorrelation function (PACF) graphs. Searching the parameters with minimum RMSE is time consuming; however, it provides indication of prediction error, which cannot be obtained by the ACF and PACF method.

The closing values for the missing days of each time series data set are completed to further reduce the RMSE error. The predicted prices after completing the missing values provided extra reduction of RMSE. The mean absolute prediction errors in data set (closing price) after filling the missing values were approximately equal or less than the mean absolute prediction errors in the data with missing values. The prediction model with the preprocessing provides more accurate future values for investment.

The best ARMA($r,m$) model which predicts the two-days-ahead future values with minimum RMSE error has been used to determine the market in which the capital shall be invested until that market gives negative future two-days-ahead return. The hypothesis of investing in multiple markets make higher profit compared to investing in a single market is tested by investing an initial $100 capital to each market, and to the highest returning market of all four markets.

In conclusion, the investment in London stock market gave the best result by raising the capital almost 200 times relative to the initial capital. However, the capital has increased only about 150 times when the capital has been invested in the highest returning market of the four global stock markets.

## 7.2 Future Work

For future research, we are recommend to apply ARMA($r,m$) model based on RMSE value as a good method for prediction the future closing price of stock market. However, there are other linear and non-linear models to test the indexes of stock market such as GARCH (Generalized Autoregressive Conditional Heteroskedasticity), NGARCH (Nonlinear GARCH), and IGARCH (Integrated GARCH). External factors that have an effect on stock market prices could not be neglected completely. Detection and analysis of external factors should be studied in the future.

# REFERENCES

[1] M. H. Seyed , Y. F. Mahmoud and M. B. Seyed , “A New Method For Stock Price Index Forecasting Using Fuzzy Time Series,” *Australian Journal of Basic and Applied Sciences,* no. 5(12), pp. 894-898, 2011 .

[2] C. Chatfield, The Analysis of Time-series: An Introduction, SIXTH ed., Chapman and Hall/CRC, 2009.

[3] R. P. Schumaker and H. Chen, “Textual Analysis of Stock Market Prediction Using Financial News Articles,” in *Americas Conference on Information Systems*, Arizona, 2006.

[4] S. Fallaw, “Modeling long -run bahavior with the fractional ARIMA model,” *Monetary Economics,* no. 29, pp. 227-302, 1992.

[5] P. J. Brockwell and R. A. Davis, Time Series: Theory and Methods, 2nd ed., Colorado State University, 1991.

[6] M. Jonas, K. Joana and K. Igor, “On autoregressive moving-average models as a tool of virtual stock-exchange : experimental investigation,” *Lietuvos matematikos rinkinys,* vol. 53, p. 129–134, 2012.

[7] L. T. J., G. A. , . D. B. M. and . D. F. A., “Forecast of hourly average wind speed with ARMA models in

Navarre (Spain)," *Solar Energy,* vol. 79, p. 65–77, 2005.

[8] A. G. Paul , "The Time-Series Behavior of Quarterly Earnings: Preliminary Evidence," *Journal of Accounting Research,* vol. 15, no. 1, pp. 71-83, 1977.

[9] . P. Ping-Feng and L. Chih-Sheng , "AhybridARIMAand support vector machines model in stock price forecasting," *Omega ,* no. 33, p. 497 – 505, 2005.

[10] . L. S. Brian, M. . W. Billy and K. . O. R. , "Comparison of parametric and nonparametric models for traffic flow forecasting," *Transportation Research Part C,* no. 10, p. 303–321, 2002.

[11] J. N. Francisco , C. Javier , J. . C. Antonio and . E. Rosario, "Forecasting Next-Day Electricity Prices by Time Series Models," *IEEE TRANSACTIONS ON POWER SYSTEMS,* vol. 17, no. 2, pp. 342-348, 2002.

[12] P. Whittle, Hypothesis Testing in Time Series Analysis, 1st ed., English Universities Press, 1951.

[13] E. P. George, M. J. Gwilym and C. R. Gregory, Time Series Analysis: Forecasting and Control, FOURTH ed.

[14] N. R. Sabri, "Stock Volatility and Market Crisis in Emerging Economies," *the American Society for Information Science,* pp. 59-83, 2004.

[15] W. P. Hamilton, The Stock Market Baraometer, Canada, 1922.

[16] R. P. Chen and Hsinchun, "The Effect of Momentum and Contrarian Stock Selection Strategies," *the American Society for Information Science,* pp. 247-255, 2008.

[17] R. Kitt and J. Kalda, Scaling analysis of multi-variants intermittent time-series, 2005, p. 480–492.

[18] "New York Stock Exchange," Wikipedia, 21 July 2013. [Online]. Available: https://en.wikipedia.org/wiki/New_York_Stock_Exchange. [Accessed 22 7 2013].

[19] "London Stock Exchange," Wikipedia, 18 July 2013. [Online]. Available: https://en.wikipedia.org/wiki/London_Stock_Exchange. [Accessed 22 7 2013].

[20] "Tokyo Stock Exchange," Wikipedia, 29 May 2013 2013. [Online]. Available: http://en.wikipedia.org/wiki/Tokyo_Stock_Exchange. [Accessed 22 7 2013].

[21] "Shanghai Stock Exchange," Wikipedia, 21 June 2013. [Online]. Available: http://en.wikipedia.org/wiki/Shanghai_Stock_Exchange. [Accessed 22 7 2013].

[22] "Wikipedia," Wikipedia, 15 9 2012. [Online]. Available:

http://en.wikipedia.org/wiki/List_of_stock_exchanges. [Accessed 16 9 2013].

[23] . J. B. Peter and A. D. Richard , Introduction to Time Series and Forecasting, 2nd ed., New York: Springer-Verlag New York, Inc, 2002.

[24] B. V. Nagendra and C. Dr. Tansen , "FORECASTING ECONOMIC TIME SERIES DATA USING ARMA," pp. 1-8.

[25] *Econometrics Toolbox™ User's Guide R2012b,* U.S.: The MathWorks, Inc., 2012, p. 241.

[26] "YAHOO! Finance," 10 1 2013. [Online]. Available: finance.yahoo.com/..

[27] Wikipedia, "Transaction," WIKIPIDIA, 27 February 2013. [Online]. Available: http://en.wikipedia.org/wiki/Transaction. [Accessed 11 9 2013].

[28] "OANDA," OANDA Corporation, [Online]. Available: http://www.oanda.com/currency/historical-rates/. [Accessed 20 3 2013].

[29] J. L. Roderick and B. R. Donald, Statistical Analysis with Missing Data, New Jersey: John wiley &sons,Inc., 2002.

[30] B. Thierry , . T. Philippe and U. Michael , "Linear Interpolation Revitalized," *IEEE TRANSACTIONS*

*ON IMAGE PROCESSING,* vol. 13, no. 5, pp. 710-719, 2004.

[31] T. Bollerslev, "A Conditionally Heteroskedastic Time Series Model for Speculative Prices and Rate of Return," *Economic and statistics,* vol. 69, no. 3, pp. 542-547, Aug 1987.

[32] K. Alan and . R. S. Hans, "Price Impacts of Block Trading on the New York Stock Exchange," *The Journal of Finance,* vol. 27, no. 3, pp. 569-588, 1972.

[33] J. W. Cort and M. Kenji , "Advantages of the mean absolute error (MAE) over," *Clim Res,* vol. 30, pp. 79-82, 19 December 2005.

[34] C. Javier , E. Rosario , J. N. Francisco and J. C. Antonio , "ARIMA Models to Predict Next-Day Electricity Prices," *IEEE TRANSACTIONS ON POWER SYSTEMS,* vol. 18, no. 3, pp. 1014-1020, AUGUST 2003.

[35] A. G. Paul , "The Time-Series Behavior of Quarterly Earnings: Preliminary Evidence," *Journal of Accounting Research,* vol. 15, no. 1, pp. 71-83, 1977.

[36] H. Akaike, "A new look at the statistical model identification," *IEEE TRANSACTIONS ON AUTOMATIC CONTROL,* Vols. AC-19,, no. 6, pp. 716-723, 1974.

[37] A. Liddle, "Information criteria for astrophysical model selection," *Mon. Not. R. Astron. Soc,* vol. 377, pp. 74-78, 19 Feb 2007.

[38] J. C. Antonio , A. P. Miguel , E. Rosa and . B. M. Ana, "Day-Ahead Electricity Price Forecasting Using the Wavelet Transform and ARIMA Models," *IEEE TRANSACTIONS ON POWER SYSTEMS,* vol. 20, no. 2, pp. 1035-1042, MAY 2005.

[39] S. Robert and A. A. George, Animal spirits: how human psychology drives the economy, and why it matters for global capitalism, Arizona: Princeton Univ Pr, 2009.

[40] N. N. Taleb, The Black Swan: Why Don't We Learn that We Don't Learn?, Las Vegas: New York University, 2008.

[41] . F. M. John, "Rational Expectations and the Theory of Price Movements," *Econometrica,* vol. 29, no. 3, pp. 315-335, Jul. 1961.

[42] K. Juseong , "The Relaxation of Financing Constraints by the Initial Public Offering of Small Manufacturing Firms," *Small Business Economics,* no. 12, p. 191–202, 1999.

[43] J. M. Keynes, The General Theory of Employment, Interest, and Money, Cambridge: King's College, Cambridge, 1936.

# APPENDIX

## Appendix A: Time Series Data Set

### A.1: NY stock market data in 2008-2012(1)

| Date | Open | High | Low | Close |
|---|---|---|---|---|
| 15/01/2008 | 1411.88 | 1411.88 | 1380.6 | 1380.95 |
| 16/01/2008 | 1377.41 | 1391.99 | 1364.27 | 1373.2 |
| 17/01/2008 | 1374.79 | 1377.72 | 1330.67 | 1333.25 |
| 18/01/2008 | 1333.9 | 1350.28 | 1312.51 | 1325.19 |
| 22/01/2008 | 1312.94 | 1322.09 | 1274.29 | 1310.5 |
| 23/01/2008 | 1310.41 | 1339.09 | 1270.05 | 1338.6 |
| 24/01/2008 | 1340.13 | 1355.15 | 1334.31 | 1352.07 |
| 25/01/2008 | 1357.32 | 1368.56 | 1327.5 | 1330.61 |
| 28/01/2008 | 1330.7 | 1353.97 | 1322.26 | 1353.96 |
| 29/01/2008 | 1355.94 | 1364.93 | 1350.19 | 1362.3 |
| 2009 | | | | |
| 15/01/2009 | 841.99 | 851.59 | 817.04 | 843.74 |
| 16/01/2009 | 844.45 | 858.13 | 830.66 | 850.12 |
| 20/01/2009 | 849.64 | 849.64 | 804.47 | 805.22 |
| 21/01/2009 | 806.77 | 841.72 | 804.3 | 840.24 |
| 22/01/2009 | 839.74 | 839.74 | 811.29 | 827.5 |
| 23/01/2009 | 822.16 | 838.61 | 806.07 | 831.95 |
| 26/01/2009 | 832.5 | 852.53 | 827.69 | 836.57 |
| 27/01/2009 | 837.3 | 850.45 | 835.4 | 845.71 |
| 28/01/2009 | 845.73 | 877.86 | 845.73 | 874.09 |

| | | | | |
|---|---|---|---|---|
| 29/01/2009 | 868.89 | 868.89 | 844.15 | 845.14 |
| 2010 | | | | |
| 15/01/2010 | 1147.72 | 1147.77 | 1131.39 | 1136.03 |
| 19/01/2010 | 1136.03 | 1150.45 | 1135.77 | 1150.23 |
| 20/01/2010 | 1147.95 | 1147.95 | 1129.25 | 1138.04 |
| 21/01/2010 | 1138.68 | 1141.58 | 1114.84 | 1116.48 |
| 22/01/2010 | 1115.49 | 1115.49 | 1090.18 | 1091.76 |
| 25/01/2010 | 1092.4 | 1102.97 | 1092.4 | 1096.78 |
| 26/01/2010 | 1095.8 | 1103.69 | 1089.86 | 1092.17 |
| 27/01/2010 | 1091.94 | 1099.51 | 1083.11 | 1097.5 |
| 28/01/2010 | 1096.93 | 1100.22 | 1078.46 | 1084.53 |
| 29/01/2010 | 1087.61 | 1096.45 | 1071.59 | 1073.87 |
| 2011 | | | | |
| 14/01/2011 | 1282.9 | 1293.24 | 1281.24 | 1293.24 |
| 18/01/2011 | 1293.22 | 1296.06 | 1290.16 | 1295.02 |
| 19/01/2011 | 1294.52 | 1294.6 | 1278.92 | 1281.92 |
| 20/01/2011 | 1280.85 | 1283.35 | 1271.26 | 1280.26 |
| 21/01/2011 | 1283.63 | 1291.21 | 1282.07 | 1283.35 |

# A.1: NY stock market data in 2008-2012(2)

| Date | Open | High | Low | Close |
|---|---|---|---|---|
| 24/01/2011 | 1283.29 | 1291.93 | 1282.47 | 1290.84 |
| 25/01/2011 | 1288.17 | 1291.26 | 1281.07 | 1291.18 |
| 26/01/2011 | 1291.97 | 1299.74 | 1291.97 | 1296.63 |
| 27/01/2011 | 1297.51 | 1301.29 | 1294.41 | 1299.54 |
| 28/01/2011 | 1299.63 | 1302.67 | 1275.1 | 1276.34 |
| 2012 | | | | |
| 17/12/2012 | 1413.54 | 1430.67 | 1413.54 | 1430.36 |
| 18/12/2012 | 1430.47 | 1448 | 1430.47 | 1446.79 |
| 19/12/2012 | 1446.79 | 1447.75 | 1435.8 | 1435.81 |
| 20/12/2012 | 1435.81 | 1443.7 | 1432.82 | 1443.69 |
| 21/12/2012 | 1443.67 | 1443.67 | 1422.58 | 1430.15 |
| 24/12/2012 | 1430.15 | 1430.15 | 1424.66 | 1426.66 |
| 26/12/2012 | 1426.66 | 1429.42 | 1416.43 | 1419.83 |
| 27/12/2012 | 1419.83 | 1422.8 | 1401.8 | 1418.1 |
| 28/12/2012 | 1418.1 | 1418.1 | 1401.58 | 1402.43 |
| 31/12/2012 | 1402.43 | 1426.74 | 1398.11 | 1426.19 |

## A.2: Sample of data in target stock market (1)

| Date | LD | TK | SH |
|---|---|---|---|
| 10/01/2008 | 12238.80636 | 128.548196 | 750.27425 |
| 11/01/2008 | 12143.516 | 122.891041 | 753.595032 |
| 12/01/2008 | 12149.55687 | 123.8702158 | 754.3837713 |
| 13/01/2008 | 12155.59775 | 124.8493905 | 755.1725107 |
| 14/01/2008 | 12161.63862 | 125.8285653 | 755.96125 |
| 15/01/2008 | 11807.1632 | 126.80774 | 749.609883 |
| 16/01/2008 | 11654.62119 | 128.909997 | 729.575119 |
| 17/01/2008 | 11575.78688 | 125.263836 | 710.92494 |
| 18/01/2008 | 11605.69305 | 116.929365 | 713.874278 |
| 19/01/2008 | 11372.06976 | 118.1506313 | 701.8166107 |
| 2009 | | | |
| 09/01/2009 | 6727.46655 | 91.979105 | 278.300046 |
| 10/01/2009 | 6721.09394 | 91.249014 | 278.080409 |
| 11/01/2009 | 6714.72133 | 90.518923 | 277.860772 |
| 12/01/2009 | 6708.34872 | 89.788832 | 277.641135 |
| 13/01/2009 | 6594.69081 | 89.058741 | 272.238357 |
| 14/01/2009 | 6131.68602 | 92.17768 | 281.807907 |
| 15/01/2009 | 6001.14582 | 92.47672 | 280.542681 |
| 16/01/2009 | 6055.18071 | 90.336848 | 285.543684 |
| 17/01/2009 | 6055.01929 | 89.19724533 | 287.0470627 |
| 18/01/2009 | 6054.85787 | 88.05764267 | 288.5504413 |
| 19/01/2009 | 6054.69645 | 86.91804 | 290.05382 |
| 2010 | | | |
| 15/01/2010 | 8889.5743 | 117.33741 | 471.693145 |
| 16/01/2010 | 8903.798227 | 117.5958467 | 472.54048 |
| 17/01/2010 | 8918.022153 | 117.8542833 | 473.387815 |

| | | | |
|---|---|---|---|
| 18/01/2010 | 8932.24608 | 118.11272 | 474.23515 |
| 19/01/2010 | 8992.41741 | 119.55251 | 475.017081 |
| 20/01/2010 | 8878.72832 | 116.49605 | 461.115655 |
| 21/01/2010 | 8696.74651 | 115.63959 | 462.141218 |
| 22/01/2010 | 8605.7084 | 113.57808 | 457.399858 |
| 23/01/2010 | 8561.394003 | 113.651416 | 455.9404467 |
| 24/01/2010 | 8517.079607 | 113.724752 | 454.4810353 |
| 2011 | | | |
| 15/01/2011 | 9480.24764 | 127.4334087 | 418.324068 |
| 16/01/2011 | 9487.98106 | 127.5871593 | 414.597528 |
| 17/01/2011 | 9495.71448 | 127.74091 | 410.870988 |
| 18/01/2011 | 9615.14064 | 126.291451 | 410.41047 |
| 19/01/2011 | 9535.82485 | 124.321692 | 418.12796 |

# A.2: Sample of data in target stock market (2)

| Date | LD | TK | SH |
|---|---|---|---|
| 21/01/2011 | 9399.88146 | 126.619482 | 411.637964 |
| 22/01/2011 | 9435.28073 | 126.367318 | 410.9185987 |
| 23/01/2011 | 9470.68 | 126.115154 | 410.1992333 |
| 24/01/2011 | 9506.07927 | 125.86299 | 409.479868 |
| 2012 | | | |
| 22/12/2012 | 9647.875907 | 121.758754 | 341.961592 |
| 23/12/2012 | 9636.717813 | 121.776224 | 341.977556 |
| 24/12/2012 | 9625.55972 | 121.793694 | 341.99352 |
| 25/12/2012 | 9618.666923 | 121.811164 | 350.857185 |
| 26/12/2012 | 9611.774127 | 122.663124 | 351.732105 |
| 27/12/2012 | 9604.88133 | 122.663124 | 349.63515 |
| 28/12/2012 | 9561.81798 | 122.663124 | 353.523475 |
| 29/12/2012 | 9550.117433 | 122.663124 | 355.416743 |
| 30/12/2012 | 9538.416887 | 122.663124 | 357.310011 |
| 31/12/2012 | 9526.71634 | 122.663124 | 359.203279 |

## Appendix B
## The currency rate with dollar 2008-2012 (1)

| Date | CNY/USD | GBP/USD | JPY/USD |
|---|---|---|---|
| 15/01/2008 | 0.1377 | 1.9595 | 0.0092 |
| 16/01/2008 | 0.1379 | 1.9611 | 0.0093 |
| 17/01/2008 | 0.138 | 1.9612 | 0.0094 |
| 18/01/2008 | 0.1378 | 1.9665 | 0.0093 |
| 19/01/2008 | 0.1379 | 1.9643 | 0.0093 |
| 20/01/2008 | 0.1379 | 1.9549 | 0.0094 |
| 21/01/2008 | 0.1379 | 1.9549 | 0.0094 |
| 22/01/2008 | 0.1379 | 1.9503 | 0.0094 |
| 23/01/2008 | 0.138 | 1.9475 | 0.0094 |
| 24/01/2008 | 0.1381 | 1.9561 | 0.0094 |
| 2009 | | | |
| 13/01/2009 | 0.1461 | 1.4991 | 0.0111 |
| 14/01/2009 | 0.1461 | 1.4667 | 0.0112 |
| 15/01/2009 | 0.1461 | 1.4562 | 0.0112 |
| 16/01/2009 | 0.1461 | 1.4601 | 0.0112 |
| 17/01/2009 | 0.1461 | 1.4792 | 0.0111 |
| 18/01/2009 | 0.146 | 1.4728 | 0.011 |
| 19/01/2009 | 0.146 | 1.4737 | 0.011 |
| 20/01/2009 | 0.1461 | 1.4695 | 0.011 |
| 21/01/2009 | 0.146 | 1.412 | 0.0111 |
| 22/01/2009 | 0.146 | 1.3841 | 0.0112 |
| 2010 | | | |
| 15/01/2010 | 0.1463 | 1.6295 | 0.0109 |
| 16/01/2010 | 0.1463 | 1.63 | 0.011 |
| 17/01/2010 | 0.1465 | 1.6259 | 0.011 |
| 18/01/2010 | 0.1465 | 1.6257 | 0.011 |

| | | | |
|---|---|---|---|
| 19/01/2010 | 0.1463 | 1.6311 | 0.011 |
| 20/01/2010 | 0.1463 | 1.6379 | 0.011 |
| 21/01/2010 | 0.1463 | 1.6301 | 0.011 |
| 22/01/2010 | 0.1462 | 1.6228 | 0.011 |
| 23/01/2010 | 0.1463 | 1.618 | 0.0111 |
| 24/01/2010 | 0.1463 | 1.61 | 0.0111 |
| 2011 | | | |
| 15/01/2011 | 0.1515 | 1.5848 | 0.0121 |
| 16/01/2011 | 0.1517 | 1.5864 | 0.0121 |
| 17/01/2011 | 0.1518 | 1.5864 | 0.0121 |
| 18/01/2011 | 0.1515 | 1.5876 | 0.0121 |
| 19/01/2011 | 0.1516 | 1.5955 | 0.0121 |
| 20/01/2011 | 0.1517 | 1.5992 | 0.0122 |
| 21/01/2011 | 0.1516 | 1.5942 | 0.0121 |
| 22/01/2011 | 0.1517 | 1.5936 | 0.0121 |

# Appendix B: The currency rate with dollar 2008-2012 (2)

| Date | CNY/USD | GBP/USD | JPY/USD | Date |
|---|---|---|---|---|
| 23/01/2011 | 0.1517 | 1.5995 | 0.0121 | 23/01/2011 |
| 24/01/2011 | 0.1519 | 1.5993 | 0.0121 | 24/01/2011 |
| | | 2012 | | |
| 22/12/2012 | 0.1586 | 1.6229 | 0.0119 | 22/12/2012 |
| 23/12/2012 | 0.1584 | 1.6167 | 0.0119 | 23/12/2012 |
| 24/12/2012 | 0.1584 | 1.6166 | 0.0119 | 24/12/2012 |
| 25/12/2012 | 0.1585 | 1.6159 | 0.0118 | 25/12/2012 |
| 26/12/2012 | 0.1585 | 1.6132 | 0.0118 | 26/12/2012 |
| 27/12/2012 | 0.1585 | 1.6131 | 0.0118 | 27/12/2012 |
| 28/12/2012 | 0.1583 | 1.6137 | 0.0117 | 28/12/2012 |
| 29/12/2012 | 0.1584 | 1.6122 | 0.0116 | 29/12/2012 |
| 30/12/2012 | 0.1583 | 1.6153 | 0.0116 | 30/12/2012 |

# Appendix C
# Sample of data forecasting by ARMA(r,m) model (1)

| Date | LD p | NY p | SHp | TKp | LNr | NY r | SH r | TK r |
|---|---|---|---|---|---|---|---|---|
| 01/01/2010 | 8789.054 | 1125.299 | 478.7512 | 115.7822 | 0.009658 | 0.006559 | -0.00098 | -0.00166 |
| 02/01/2010 | 8874.354 | 1132.703 | 478.2804 | 115.5897 | 0.003915 | 0.005332 | -0.00527 | -0.00416 |
| 03/01/2010 | 8909.16 | 1138.759 | 475.7648 | 115.1093 | 0.002798 | 0.010662 | -0.00115 | 0.000944 |
| 04/01/2010 | 8934.121 | 1150.965 | 475.2196 | 115.2181 | 0.001004 | -0.00399 | 0.008315 | 0.001776 |
| 05/01/2010 | 8943.095 | 1146.387 | 479.1875 | 115.4228 | 0.004662 | 0.009776 | -0.00091 | 5.82E-05 |
| 06/01/2010 | 8984.887 | 1157.649 | 478.7534 | 115.4295 | -0.01947 | -0.00649 | -0.02677 | 0.027083 |
| 07/01/2010 | 8811.62 | 1150.164 | 466.1087 | 118.5984 | -0.00372 | 0.009586 | -0.00224 | -0.00131 |
| 08/01/2010 | 8778.894 | 1161.243 | 465.0677 | 118.4436 | 0.013034 | -0.00499 | 0.006327 | -0.01876 |
| 09/01/2010 | 8894.067 | 1155.459 | 468.0197 | 116.2426 | 0.004923 | 0.005357 | -0.00169 | -0.00177 |
| 10/01/2010 | 8937.964 | 1161.665 | 467.228 | 116.0372 | -0.00361 | -0.00847 | 0.003278 | 0.01028 |
| 11/01/2010 | 8905.737 | 1151.873 | 468.7621 | 117.2362 | 0.001366 | 0.004389 | -0.00122 | 0.002587 |

| | | | | | | | | |
|---|---|---|---|---|---|---|---|---|
| 12/01/2010 | 8917.91 | 1156.94 | 468.1921 | 117.5399 | -0.00838 | -0.00436 | -0.00716 | 0.017045 |
| 13/01/2010 | 8843.481 | 1151.909 | 464.852 | 119.5605 | 0.002951 | 0.006535 | -0.00363 | -0.00238 |
| 14/01/2010 | 8869.615 | 1159.461 | 463.1671 | 119.2765 | 0.003948 | -0.01561 | 0.016362 | -0.01802 |
| 15/01/2010 | 8904.704 | 1141.503 | 470.8079 | 117.1463 | 0.001159 | 0.005018 | -0.00061 | -0.00083 |
| 16/01/2010 | 8915.027 | 1147.245 | 470.5205 | 117.0495 | -0.00017 | 0.00153 | 0.003231 | 0.006059 |
| 17/01/2010 | 8913.534 | 1149.002 | 472.0431 | 117.7609 | 0.001159 | 0.009663 | -0.00196 | -0.00072 |
| 18/01/2010 | 8923.87 | 1160.158 | 471.1188 | 117.676 | 0.015198 | -0.00275 | 0.00951 | 0.017879 |
| 19/01/2010 | 9060.534 | 1156.966 | 475.6205 | 119.7989 | 0.00397 | 0.008777 | -0.00018 | -0.00034 |
| 2011 | | | | | | | | |
| 01/01/2011 | 9021.2 | 1249.268 | 424.2196 | 126.8941 | 0.026413 | 0.013675 | 0.00046 | 0.00858 |
| 02/01/2011 | 9262.655 | 1266.469 | 424.4145 | 127.9875 | 0.003463 | -0.00211 | 0.00066 | -0.00332 |
| 03/01/2011 | 9294.787 | 1263.8 | 424.6945 | 127.5635 | 0.003404 | 0.003022 | 0.017877 | 0.014422 |
| 04/01/2011 | 9326.48 | 1267.626 | 432.3551 | 129.4166 | -0.00599 | -0.00297 | -0.00092 | -0.00232 |
| 05/01/2011 | 9270.778 | 1263.862 | 431.9564 | 129.1168 | 0.008319 | 0.004817 | -0.0127 | -0.01767 |

| | | | | | | | | |
|---|---|---|---|---|---|---|---|---|
| 06/01/2011 | 9348.22 | 1269.966 | 426.506 | 126.8552 | -0.00432 | -0.00314 | -0.00098 | -0.00126 |
| 07/01/2011 | 9307.884 | 1265.983 | 426.0864 | 126.6953 | -0.01335 | 0.000332 | 0.000123 | -0.00312 |
| 08/01/2011 | 9184.428 | 1266.403 | 426.1389 | 126.3003 | -0.00672 | -0.00514 | -0.00103 | 0.001982 |
| 09/01/2011 | 9122.936 | 1259.914 | 425.7022 | 126.5508 | 0.015162 | 0.003315 | -0.01457 | 0.002551 |
| 10/01/2011 | 9262.312 | 1264.098 | 419.5434 | 126.8741 | -0.00215 | -0.00613 | -0.001 | 6.48E-05 |
| 11/01/2011 | 9242.453 | 1256.373 | 419.1231 | 126.8823 | 0.020307 | 0.02215 | 0.015934 | -0.00815 |
| 12/01/2011 | 9432.055 | 1284.513 | 425.8551 | 125.8525 | 0.001196 | -0.00331 | -0.00074 | -0.00045 |
| 13/01/2011 | 9443.346 | 1280.263 | 425.542 | 125.7955 | 0.002333 | 0.007885 | -0.00923 | 0.012127 |
| 14/01/2011 | 9465.402 | 1290.398 | 421.6328 | 127.3303 | -0.00767 | -0.00307 | -0.00109 | -0.00103 |
| 15/01/2011 | 9393.113 | 1286.445 | 421.1728 | 127.1991 | 0.006608 | 0.003704 | -0.01683 | 0.002446 |
| 16/01/2011 | 9455.392 | 1291.219 | 414.1431 | 127.5106 | -0.00681 | -0.0039 | -0.00174 | -0.00074 |
| 17/01/2011 | 9391.176 | 1286.195 | 413.4236 | 127.4168 | 0.022379 | 0.003381 | -0.01068 | -0.01162 |
| 18/01/2011 | 9603.71 | 1290.551 | 409.0298 | 125.9447 | -0.00269 | -0.0047 | -0.002 | -0.00075 |

| | | | | | | | | |
|---|---|---|---|---|---|---|---|---|
| 19/01/2011 | 9577.892 | 1284.497 | 408.2143 | 125.8498 | -0.03453 | -0.01156 | -0.00426 | 0.003159 |
| 2012 | | | | | | | | |
| 11/12/2012 | 9381.942 | 1382.928 | 331.2747 | 116.0006 | 0.018504 | 0.022812 | 0.00062 | 0.015257 |

# Appendix C
# Sample of data forecasting by ARMA(*r*,*m*) model (2)

| Date | LD p | NY p | SHp | TKp | LNr | NY r | SH r | TK r |
|---|---|---|---|---|---|---|---|---|
| 12/12/2012 | 9557.164 | 1414.838 | 331.4803 | 117.784 | -0.00469 | -0.01269 | 0.00266 | -0.00225 |
| 13/12/2012 | 9512.412 | 1397.002 | 332.3631 | 117.519 | -0.00101 | -0.00159 | 0.03026 | 0.012739 |
| 14/12/2012 | 9502.816 | 1394.778 | 342.574 | 119.0257 | -0.00976 | -0.01562 | 0.004845 | -0.00293 |
| 15/12/2012 | 9410.549 | 1373.165 | 344.2379 | 118.6773 | 0.012085 | 0.025933 | -0.00238 | 0.018016 |
| 16/12/2012 | 9524.966 | 1409.242 | 343.4203 | 120.8348 | -0.00577 | -0.01377 | 0.001257 | -0.00183 |
| 17/12/2012 | 9470.165 | 1389.973 | 343.8523 | 120.6142 | 0.012243 | 0.030942 | 0.002275 | -0.01259 |
| 18/12/2012 | 9586.822 | 1433.655 | 344.6355 | 119.1056 | -0.00891 | -0.01423 | 0.002026 | -0.00183 |
| 19/12/2012 | 9501.744 | 1413.4 | 345.3343 | 118.8875 | 0.019465 | 0.008403 | -0.0031 | 0.008488 |
| 20/12/2012 | 9688.506 | 1425.326 | 344.2669 | 119.9009 | -0.008 | -0.01493 | -0.00015 | -0.00007 |
| 21/12/2012 | 9611.312 | 1404.207 | 344.2163 | 119.8922 | -0.00467 | 0.0082 | -0.00362 | 0.016871 |
| 22/12/2012 | 9566.505 | 1415.769 | 342.9717 | 121.9321 | -0.01149 | -0.01427 | 1.54E-03 | -0.00095 |

| | | | | | | | | |
|---|---|---|---|---|---|---|---|---|
| 23/12/2012 | 9457.225 | 1395.706 | 343.5016 | 121.8157 | 0.01367 | 0.008914 | -0.003 | -0.00312 |
| 24/12/2012 | 9587.393 | 1408.203 | 342.4057 | 121.4361 | -0.0086 | -0.01523 | 5.02E-04 | -0.00219 |
| 25/12/2012 | 9505.303 | 1386.916 | 342.5775 | 121.1701 | 0.003981 | 0.0066 | 0.028793 | 0.012903 |
| 26/12/2012 | 9543.223 | 1396.1 | 352.5849 | 122.7437 | -0.00931 | -0.01682 | 0.001678 | -0.00091 |
| 27/12/2012 | 9454.772 | 1372.808 | 353.177 | 122.6325 | 0.006794 | 0.006736 | 0.002066 | -0.00174 |
| 28/12/2012 | 9519.222 | 1382.087 | 353.9074 | 122.4198 | -0.00968 | -0.01706 | 0.002493 | -0.00122 |
| 29/12/2012 | 9427.537 | 1358.714 | 354.7909 | 122.2709 | 0.006158 | 0.03441 | 0.008607 | 0.002541 |

# Appendix D
# Investment date, stock market, and value

| Date | LD p | NY p | SHp | TKp | LNr | NY r | SHr | TKr | Mb | Ms | shr b | shr s | inv b | Inv s |
|---|---|---|---|---|---|---|---|---|---|---|---|---|---|---|
| 15/01/2010 | 8904.704 | 1141.503 | 470.8079 | 117.1463 | 0.001159 | 0.005018 | -0.00061 | -0.00083 | NY | | 0.09 | 0 | 102.7551 | 0 |
| 16/01/2010 | 8915.027 | 1147.245 | 470.5205 | 117.0495 | -0.00017 | 0.00153 | 0.003231 | 0.006059 | | NY | 0 | 0.090017 | 0 | 103.272 |
| 19/01/2010 | 9060.534 | 1156.966 | 475.6205 | 119.7989 | 0.00397 | 0.008777 | -0.00018 | -0.00034 | NY | | 0.089 | 0 | 103.272 | 0 |
| 20/01/2010 | 9096.572 | 1167.165 | 475.5363 | 119.7582 | -0.05915 | -0.04275 | -0.03429 | -0.0375 | | NY | 0 | 0.089261 | 0 | 104.1824 |
| 21/01/2010 | 8574.087 | 1118.32 | 459.5071 | 115.3501 | -0.0075 | -0.00029 | -0.00106 | 0.001926 | TK | | 0.9 | 0 | 104.1824 | 0 |
| 22/01/2010 | 8509.995 | 1117.999 | 459.0213 | 115.5725 | 0.007327 | -0.01618 | -0.00878 | -0.01736 | | TK | 0 | 0.903184 | 0 | 104.3833 |
| 23/01/2010 | 8572.58 | 1100.06 | 455.0099 | 113.5833 | 0.011975 | 0.009336 | -0.00342 | 0.005569 | LD | | 0.012176 | 0 | 104.3833 | 0 |
| 26/01/2010 | 8489.874 | 1114.2 | 452.2312 | 114.0694 | 0.005727 | -0.00957 | -0.03776 | -0.00646 | | LD | 0 | 0.012176 | 0 | 103.3762 |
| 27/01/2010 | 8538.638 | 1103.593 | 435.4727 | 113.3344 | 0.011715 | 0.010036 | -0.00399 | -0.00139 | LD | | 0.012107 | 0 | 103.3762 | 0 |
| 28/01/2010 | 8639.258 | 1114.724 | 433.7396 | 113.177 | -0.02365 | -0.02736 | 0.006883 | 0.019178 | | LD | 0 | 0.012107 | 0 | 104.5944 |
| 2011 | | | | | | | | | | | | | | |
| 14/12/2011 | 8346.927 | 1208.683 | 347.8211 | 107.7365 | 0.003334 | -0.00566 | -0.00011 | 0.000522 | LD | | 0.257438 | 0 | 2148.817 | 0 |
| 15/12/2011 | 8374.805 | 1201.857 | 347.7817 | 107.7928 | -8.19E-03 | 0.018948 | -0.00342 | -0.00806 | | LD | 0 | 0.257438 | 0 | 2155.994 |
| 16/12/2011 | 8306.523 | 1224.848 | 346.5929 | 106.927 | 0.016285 | 0.00346 | 0.000213 | 0.003805 | LD | | 0.259554 | 0 | 2155.994 | 0 |
| 17/12/2011 | 8442.906 | 1229.093 | 346.6666 | 107.3346 | -0.00156 | -0.02552 | -0.00054 | 0.005748 | | LD | 0 | 0.259554 | 0 | 2191.393 |

| | | | | | | | | | | | | | | |
|---|---|---|---|---|---|---|---|---|---|---|---|---|---|---|
| 20/12/2011 | 8458.106 | 1246.005 | 347.7359 | 107.359 | 0.02084 | 0.006151 | 0.001086 | -0.00029 | LD | | 0.259088 | 0 | 2191.393 | 0 |
| 21/12/2011 | 8636.226 | 1253.694 | 348.1138 | 107.3277 | 0.001137 | 0.006767 | -0.01625 | 0.005377 | | LD | 0 | 0.259088 | 0 | 2237.542 |
| 22/12/2011 | 8646.05 | 1262.206 | 342.502 | 107.9063 | 0.014197 | 0.002026 | -0.00157 | -0.00088 | LD | | 0.258794 | 0 | 2237.542 | 0 |
| 23/12/2011 | 8769.677 | 1264.766 | 341.9637 | 107.8112 | -0.0141 | -0.00114 | 0.011464 | -0.00046 | | LD | 0 | 0.258794 | 0 | 2269.536 |
| 24/12/2011 | 8646.901 | 1263.319 | 345.9065 | 107.7618 | 0.00497 | -1.23E-03 | 0.000213 | 3.97E-05 | LD | | 0.262468 | 0 | 2269.536 | 0 |
| 29/12/2011 | 8706.916 | 1222.403 | 341.0527 | 108.2896 | -0.01045 | 0.024061 | 0.012587 | 0.010864 | | LD | 0 | 0.262468 | 0 | 2285.288 |
| 2012 | | | | | | | | | | | | | | |
| 14/12/2012 | 9502.816 | 1394.778 | 342.574 | 119.0257 | -0.00976 | -0.01562 | 0.004845 | -0.00293 | | SH | 0 | 40.41699 | 0 | 13845.81 |
| 15/12/2012 | 9410.549 | 1373.165 | 344.2379 | 118.6773 | 0.012085 | 0.025933 | -0.00238 | 0.018016 | NY | | 10.08314 | 0 | 13845.81 | 0 |
| 18/12/2012 | 9586.822 | 1433.655 | 344.6355 | 119.1056 | -0.00891 | -0.01423 | 0.002026 | -0.00183 | | NY | 0 | 10.08314 | 0 | 14455.74 |
| 19/12/2012 | 9501.744 | 1413.4 | 345.3343 | 118.8875 | 0.019465 | 0.008403 | -0.0031 | 0.008488 | LD | | 1.521377 | 0 | 14455.74 | 0 |
| 20/12/2012 | 9688.506 | 1425.326 | 344.2669 | 119.9009 | -0.008 | -0.01493 | -0.00015 | -7.28E-05 | | LD | 0 | 1.521377 | 0 | 14739.87 |
| 21/12/2012 | 9611.312 | 1404.207 | 344.2163 | 119.8922 | -0.00467 | 0.0082 | -0.00362 | 0.016871 | TK | | 122.9427 | 0 | 14739.87 | 0 |
| 22/12/2012 | 9566.505 | 1415.769 | 342.9717 | 121.9321 | -0.01149 | -0.01427 | 1.54E-03 | -0.00095 | | TK | 0 | 122.9427 | 0 | 14990.66 |
| 25/12/2012 | 9505.303 | 1386.916 | 342.5775 | 121.1701 | 0.003981 | 0.0066 | 0.028793 | 0.012903 | SH | | 43.75844 | 0 | 14990.66 | 0 |
| 28/12/2012 | 9519.222 | 1382.087 | 353.9074 | 122.4198 | -0.00968 | -0.01706 | 0.002493 | -0.00122 | | SH | 0 | 43.75844 | 0 | 15486.43 |
| 29/12/2012 | 9427.537 | 1358.714 | 354.7909 | 122.2709 | 0.006158 | 0.03441 | 0.008607 | 0.002541 | NY | | 11.39786 | 0 | 15486.43 | 0 |

# Appendix E: The source code of this work

## E.1:Pre-processing closing price

The following MATLAB codes contain pre-processing operations on the raw data of LD stock market as an example from four stock markets.

```
clc; clear all;
% London pre-processing closing price
% London preprocess.xlsx :it is excel
file contain Date %for 5 years
from(1/1/2008-31/12/2012),Date of stock
%market working day and Closing price
with missing values

[num,txt,raw] = xlsread('london
preprocess.xlsx');
N=length(raw);
Close1(N,1)=0;
for i=2:N
date_all=cell2mat(raw(i,1));
for j=2:N
date2=cell2mat(raw(j,2));
if date_all==date2
Close1(i-1,1)=num(j-1,1);
end
end
end
% Converting the closing price currency
from (GBP) to USD currency
%lndcurrency.m : if file in matlab
contain the rate of GBP currenct to USD
```

```
load lndcurrency.m;
lndusd=lndcurrency;
Close1=Close1.*lndusd;

% Using the value of next cell in each
cell have value =0, Closenext(i) are
% new Close value after substitute next
cell value
for i=1:N
if Close1(i,1)==0 &&(i+1~=N+1)&& (
Close1(i+1,1)~=0)
Closenext(i,1)=Close1(i+1,1);
else if Close1(i,1)==0 &&(i+1~=N+1)&&
(Close1(i+1,1)==0)
Closenext(i,1)=Closenext(i-1,1);
else Closenext(i,1)=Close1(i,1);
end
end
end
%use the value of previous cell in each
cell have value =0,Closepre(i)are
%new close values after substitute
previous cell value
for i=1:N
if Close1(i,1)==0 &&(i-1~=0)&&
(Close1(i-1,1)~=0)
Closepre(i,1)=Close1(i-1,1);
else if Close1(i,1)==0 &&(i-1~=0)&&
(Close1(i-1,1)==0)
Closepre(i,1)=Closepre(i-1,1);
else Closepre(i,1)=Close1(i,1);
end
end
end
```

```
%using the interpolation method in the
cell with value=0

Y = Close1(:,1);
Xi =1:length(Y);
errors = Y == 0;
X = Xi(~errors);
Y = Y(~errors);
Yi = interp1(X, Y, Xi);
% Yiv is closing price vector after
interpolation method
Yiv=Yi';
Closeinter=Yiv(:,1);
```

## E.2: Selection of best ARMA(*r*,*m*) model

The following MATLAB codes show the operation of selection the best ARMA(*r*,*m*) model in the range ARMA(1,1) to ARMA(15,15) in LD stock market

```
%% LONDON ARMA(r,m) SELECTION

clc; clear all;
% load LD closing price after pre-
processing it by interpolation method
load LNDclsint.m;
y=LNDclsint;         % y is closing price
r = price2ret(y); %r is the return of
clocing price
N=length(r);
k=0;

for i=1:15
```

```
for j=1:15
% specifying the model
model = arima(i,0,j);
%fitting reteurn according to model
specified by previous step
fit = estimate(model,r);
%spesifying the AR and MA coefficient
values
model =
arima('AR',fit.AR,'MA',fit.MA,...
'Constant',fit.Constant
,'Variance',fit.Variance);
c=1;
for d=1:2:1096  %counter for 3 years

% fitting two years data set
fit = estimate(model,r(d:730+d));
%RMSE is prediction root mean square
error for each model
%Yf is the forecasting 3 years return
price

[Yf(c:c+1,j+k)  RMSE(c:c+1,j+k)] =
forecast(fit,2,'Y0',r(d:730+d));

c=c+2;

end

if i>=100 && j>=100
f(j+k,:)=[num2str(i),'.',num2str(j)];
elseif
((((i>=10)&&(i<100))&&(j>=100))||((i>=1
00)&&((j>=10)&&(j<100))))
```

```
f(j+k,:)=[num2str(i),'.',num2str(j),'
'];
elseif((i<10&&j>=100)||((i>=10&&i<100)&
&(j>=10&&j<100))||...
(i>=100&&j<10))
f(j+k,:)=[num2str(i),'.',num2str(j),'
'];
elseif ((i<10 && (j>=10&&
j<100))||((i>=10&&(i<100))&&j<10))
f(j+k,:)=[num2str(i),'.',num2str(j),'
'];
elseif i<10 && j<10
f(j+k,:)=[num2str(i),'.',num2str(j),'
'];
end

end
k=k+j;

end

% plotting the models, x-axis contain
the ARMA(1,1)to ARMA(15,15)
%y-axis contain values of RMASE for
corresponding to the models
figure();
plot(1:k,min(RMSE),'r-o');
set(gca,'XTick',1:k);
set(gca,'XTickLabel',{f});
xlabel('ARMA(r,m) model');
ylabel(' RMSE in LD');
grid on;

save('LNDarmaselection2');
```

## E.3: Forecasting two –days-ahead using best ARMA(*r*,*m*) model

The codes below show the forecasting of two –days-ahead according to minimum RMSE value

```
%ARMA FITTING of LONDON STOCK MARKET
% load LD closing price after pre-
processing it by interpolation method
load LNDclsint.m;
y=LNDclsint;
r=price2ret(y);
N=length(y);
autocorr(r); %Autocorrelation function
parcorr(r);  %partial autocorrelation
function
%The best ARMA model is ARMA(7,8)in LD
stock market
model = arima(7,0,8);
%fitting the closing price using
ARMA(7,8) model
fit = estimate(model,y);

%specifying the AR value and MA value

model =
arima('AR',fit.AR,'MA',fit.MA,...
'Constant',fit.Constant
,'Variance',fit.Variance);

c=1;
for d=1:2:1096  % counter to forecast 3
years
```

```
fit = estimate(model,y(d:730+d)); %
fitting two years data set
%forcasting 2 days ahead based on its
previous 2 years closing price,
%RMSE is root mean squar error
%Yf is the forecasting 3 years closing
price
% E is the error ralated with MA part

[Yf(c:c+1,1)  RMSE(c:c+1,1)] =
forecast(fit,2,'Y0',y(d:730+d));
[E,V] = infer(model,y(d:730+d));

c=c+2;
end
% plotting the actual and forecasting
price
figure();
[num,txt,raw] =
xlsread('dateto2012.xlsx');
h1 =plot(y,'Color',[.7,.7,.7]);
hold on
h2 = plot(731:N,Yf,'b','LineWidth',1);
set(gca,'XTick',[1:365:N]);
set(gca,'XTickLabel',cell2mat(raw(1:365
:N)));
xlabel('(2008-2012) Period ');
ylabel('Closing Price');
legend([h1
h2],'Observed','Forecast','Location','N
orthWest');
hold off;
grid on;
```

```
%obtaining the absolute prediction
error in London stock market

abser=abs(y(731:end,1)-Yf(:,1));

%m contain the mean of absolute
prediction error

m=mean(abser);

% plotting the absolute prediction
error in London stock market
plot(abser);
set(gca,'XTick',[1:365:1096]);
set(gca,'XTickLabel',cell2mat(raw(1:365
:1096)));
grid on;
xlabel('(2010-2012) Period ');
ylabel('The Error in price (USD)');

save('LND ARMA(7,8)fitting');
```

## Appendix E.4: Investment operation in stock markets

The following codes show the investment operation in each stock market separately and investment money among stock markets in the same time. Initial value of investment is $100.

```
%The Investment: The selling and buying
operation among stock markets.
```

```
%STOCKFORECAST3yprmis.xlsx: excel file
contain price and return of
%stock market for (2010-2012) period

[num,txt,raw] =
xlsread('STOCKFORECAST3yprmis.xlsx');
buy(1,1)=100; sel(1,1)=0;
b=1;
s=2;
for i=1:2:755
mxr(i,1)=max(num(i,5:8)); %find MAX
return
[ro,co] = find(num==max(num(i,5:8)));
if co==5
bsname(b,:)='LD'; % LD=London stock
market
elseif co==6
bsname(b,:)='NY'; % NY= New York
elseif co==7
bsname(b,:)='SH'; %SH=Shanghai
else
bsname(b,:)='TK'; %TK= Tokyo
end
% sharb(b,1)=the number of shares that
have been purchased
% bsname(b,:)= contains the stock
market where purchased
%ssname(s,:)= contains the stock market
name where selling
sharb(b,1)=buy(b,1)/num(i,((co(1,1))-
4));
ssname(s,:) =bsname(b,:);
```

```
%sel(s,1)=amount of yield from selling
of shares
% shars(s,1)=the number of shares that
have been sold
sel(s,1)=sharb(b,1)*num(i+1,((co(1,1))-
4));
shars(s,1)=sharb(b,1);
b=b+2;
%buy(b,1)=the amount of mony to
purchase shares
buy(b,1)=sel(s,1);
s=s+2;
end

save('invtbtweenstock');
%%%%%%%%%%%%%%%%%%%%%%%%%%%%%%%%%
%%%%%%%%%%%
Invest in LD stock market
%STOCKFORECAST3yprmis.xlsx: excel file
contain price and return of
%stock market for (2010-2012)priod
[num,txt,raw] =
xlsread('STOCKFORECAST3yprmis.xlsx');
buy(1,1)=100;sharb(1,1)=buy(1,1)/num(1,
1);shars(1,1)=0; sel(1,1)=0; b=2;
s=2;
for i=2:754
if num(i,5)> 0 && sharb(b-1,1)==0
%%buying process

sharb(b,1)=sel(s-1,1)/num(i,1);
sel(s,1)=0;
shars(s,1)=0;
buy(b,1)=sel(s-1,1);
```

```
else
if  num(i,5)> 0 && sharb(b-1,1)~=0
sharb(b,1)=sharb(b-1,1);
buy(b,1)=buy(b-1,1);
sel(s,1)=0;
shars(s,1)=0;
end
end

if num(i,5)<0 && sharb(b-1,1)~=0
%%selling process
sel(s,1)=sharb(b-1,1)*num(i,1);
shars(s,1)=sharb(b-1,1);
sharb(b,1)=0;
buy(b,1)=0;
else if num(i,5)<0 && sharb(b-1,1)==0
sel(s,1)=sel(s-1,1);
shars(s,1)=shars(s-1,1);
sharb(b,1)=0;
buy(b,1)=0;
end
end
b=b+1;
s=s+1;
end
% save the variable value in file name
'invLD'
save('invtLD');
```

United Scholars Publications

Email: info@unitedscholars.net
www.unitedscholars.net

Printed in Dunstable, United Kingdom

91218904R00067